MW01515112

The Mothering Heights

MANUAL FOR
MOTHERHOOD

VOLUME 1

What we wish we knew before becoming a

~~short order cook~~
~~shuttle driver~~
~~laundress~~

Mother

Edited by Christine Fugate

Columnist and Creator of Mothering Heights

MH
press

Mothering Heights Press
Laguna Beach, CA

The Mothering Heights Manual for Motherhood Volume 1
Edited by Christine Fugate

Published by Mothering Heights Press.
1278 Glenneyre Street, #242
Laguna Beach, CA 92651-3103

Mothering Heights is a registered trademark

For individual essay copyright information, please see pages
146-147.

ISBN: 978-0-9817576-0-5

Printed in the United States of America on acid-free paper
Typeset in Adobe Garmond Pro, Myriad Pro, Mrs Blackfort

Book Design and Illustrations by Graphic Muse Design

for
Caterina &
Sara Jeanne

Contents

Introduction:
Beyond Tender Love
by Christine Fugate

Ever since I had my first baby at six years old, I wanted to be a mother. And why not? My Baby Tender Love doll never cried when I changed her diapers or put her down for a nap. She would lay in her tiny pink cradle with her eyes closed, nary a peep emitting from her soft pink lips. Motherhood was pure bliss. Nurturing without noise.

After giving birth to my daughter, I expected the baby bliss to pick up where I left off. But there I was, a beached whale with engorged breasts, a crying baby and no idea what to do next. To say I was lost and confused would be an understatement. And before I knew it, I was pregnant with my second child. Wasn't breastfeeding a form of birth control? Why hadn't anyone told me that motherhood would be so hard?

When it came time to pick the topic for this year's Mother's Day Essay Contest, I chose the question, "What do you know now that you wish you knew before becoming a parent?" I wanted to know from other moms what they thought was shocking, strange and completely unpredictable about motherhood. I knew there had to be more than just how hard it is.

Over one hundred essays poured in from 26 states and four countries. Reading the essays shed light on the current state of the mom-mind. For example, the word 'perfect' (or a variation of it) was used over 92 times. That's almost one 'perfect' for every mom. While I think the questioning of perfection is positive (although not every essay questioned it), the frequency shows that the desire to be 'perfect' continues to loom over our sense of identity.

In addition, I realized that criticizing motherhood makes us nervous. Many of the essays began as sharp and examining, but ended with an overly sweet tone, as if concluding on a dark note was against the mommy rules. I have struggled with this in my own writing. The fear of appearing ungrateful or uncaring towards our children and family terrifies us into using clichéd phrases and sweet endings. Hopefully, this will begin to change as we give ourselves permission to critique motherhood in our writing and conversations.

These observations made me realize what I have always suspected: The real mommy war is not between moms, but inside ourselves. We need to stop fighting the ideals and be more accepting of our messes, mistakes and mommy blues. That said every essay submitted touched my heart with its observations of modern motherhood. I laughed, cried and dreamt about the women and their stories for weeks.

As for me, what I wish I had known before I became

a parent is something my grandmother taught me long ago: This too shall pass. Just when I am about to pull my hair out, strand by strand, because of the whining about wearing tennis shoes to school or taking a bath, my daughters switch into happy mode and do whatever I ask.

This 'passing' also applies to my own self-image as a parent and a woman. Recently, I decided I was a fraud. I was writing a column about motherhood even though I was a horrible parent who would have to contribute every last dollar to my children's therapy fund. Then lo and behold, my youngest showered me with kisses as I got a call that my oldest had just been named Student of the Month. I told my husband, "Either we're doing something right or we're just plain lucky."

There are no instructions for parenthood. That is why I named this book, *The Manual for Motherhood*, as if there could be such a thing. We each have our own experiences, genetic mapping and circumstances that govern how we chose to parent.

I hope this book will be like a cup of hot chocolate, swaddling you with warm, honest voices of mothers who are telling us what they have learned, what they have experienced. These stories can guide us back to a place of knowing why we started this crazy journey called Motherhood in the first place.

Chapter 1:

Madness and Mayhem

I Love You Like the Crazy You Drive Me

by Anne Glamore

I scooped the neatly folded clothes from the laundry basket, marched over to my twelve-year-old, and dumped them over his head.

"Haven't I asked you to put these up?" I asked. I stomped on Finn's beloved Abercrombie shirt. "I do laundry every damn day!" I bent down, pulled a pair of boxers out of the pile and threw the underwear at him, hitting him in the glasses. "Why do I bother? You're driving me crazy. You can wear dirty clothes for all I care."

Finn began sobbing, either from the unexpected cussing or the indignity of being zinged by a pair of Fruit-of-the-Looms. I stood in the middle of the den, breathing heavily, and watched as he ran to his room.

"My God," I thought to myself, "is this what mothers *do*?"

I certainly didn't envision such scenes when I became pregnant. The baby inside me seemed hypothetical and easily managed. But now that my oldest boy is twelve and his twin brothers are nine, I realize that actual flesh and blood kids present new challenges every day.

In my experience, motherhood has been a lot like the song

that Dolly Parton sang: *"It's enough to drive you crazy if you let it."* Sometimes you can't help going batty. The boys have left the milk out on the counter for the millionth time, your Sharpie is gone, you locate the "lost" jacket in the closet, exactly where you told the owner it would be.

But other times mothering these brothers is a kick-ass adventure, full of shocking revelations about the essence of boys. The only way to discover that part, however, is to keep the crazy from sticking to you like dryer lint and look for the lessons in everyday events.

Pre-children, I never suspected that "mom" was a synonym for "veterinarian." Now I'm a font of esoteric animal-related information. A goldfish *can* live in water diluted with the breakfast milk. A boy *will not* die from drinking water from the fishbowl with a straw. Parakeets *can* be bathed in the potty, but that doesn't mean they should be.

It should have been obvious, but my boys had to teach me that a male's idea of interior decoration is different from a mother's. The nurseries I'd decorated in cunning pastels underwent radical changes. The boys replaced expensively framed animal prints with cheap posters of baseball players and musicians taped onto the walls without regard for the integrity of the paint underneath. Porter purchased an orange and black "NO TRESPASSING" sign from the hardware store and nailed it to his door. I sighed and began knocking before entering.

Ten years ago I had no clue that males' obsession with fire and bosoms starts at such a young age. Just last week the twins each had a friend over, and although I thought I was watching them, they managed to sneak out of the house with a pack of matches. I nabbed them as they were setting leaves on fire in the driveway. After I confiscated the matches I found the boys looking through our book on Leonardo da Vinci, but they weren't admiring his drawings of a Renaissance helicopter. They were giggling insanely at his masterly paintings that included bare-breasted ladies.

Nor did I guess that teaching the boys about reproduction would require me to summon my most down to earth talk, as well as my substantial skill at charades. My rendition of "the talk" includes the phrase "hard as a stick" and requires me to form a circle with my left hand and poke my right index finger in and out of the circle, using the international sign for coitus, to make sure the sex student completely understands how the anatomical parts fit together. It's been a big hit so far, although I suppose I won't know how successful it is until I actually hold a grandchild in my arms.

One of the most important lessons I've learned as a mother is one that you learn early on as a child: to treat others as you wish to be treated. To that end, I smother them with hugs, I remind myself to say "I love you," and I try to remember to ask for forgiveness when I scream about the latest transgression, even if it's one we've dealt with more times than I can count.

After the laundry-throwing incident, I cooled off a while and then ventured into Finn's room.

"I'm sorry I threw your underwear at you," I said. I knelt

down and gave him a hug.

"That's okay," he said. "I should have put up my clothes."

We sat there for several moments, arms and shoulders entwined, knowing that everything was cool between us. Or as he would say, "Things were poppin'."

Moves, Babies, Moments of Madness
by Kate Hasenauer

Most days begin at five a.m. and end after midnight when the baby finally falls asleep in mid-shriek. I cringe thinking about the total disorganization that is my life right now, but I am calmed by the sight of the children sound asleep with their innocent faces poking out from beneath the covers. I sit on the couch with a glass of flat wine and see how long I can stay awake or until a tiny voice says, "Momma, I am going to throw up."

My children are four, two and five months old. We've moved five times since my first pregnancy. So aside from sleep deprivation and exhaustion from being home with three children, there are days when I am not sure what city we're in.

After our first pregnancy test came back positive, my husband, Jim, announced that he was probably sterile.

Nine months later in Birmingham, Alabama, Henry was born. We thought he was a miracle and could be our only one. He was hardly put down.

My mother commented, "You seem to pick him up before he gets a chance to cry."

She'd told me that it was good for a baby to cry, but I didn't take her advice because she'd propped my baby bottle up with a stuffed dog rather than feeding me herself.

Anabel, our second, was born in Mission Viejo, California. Jim couldn't believe that we'd conceived again because he'd been exposed to radiation while working in a lab. Wrong again.

Our daughter came out screaming and hasn't stopped talking since. If someone had told me to imagine having a child exactly like my husband, my response would have been, "I can't handle that!"

During a wildly frustrating month, I started taking anti-anxiety medication and was excited about the prospect of becoming a calm mother. A few days into taking the medicine, I had an aluminum taste in my mouth.

In a panic, I darted to the pharmacy with Jim yelling behind me, "There is no way in hell."

I bought the least expensive pregnancy test available and some M&Ms and cried on the toilet while watching the two pink lines appear. The next day, the children went with me to K-Mart. I whispered to a clerk to direct me to the early pregnancy tests.

The clerk yelled through the store, "Show this woman the pregnancy tests."

I stood there, cowering, and hoped no one would see me. Why would I have another child? My children bit each other, hit each other and ran away in crowded parking lots. I clearly wasn't doing enough right to warrant a third. We were done at two, but at forty-two and thirty-seven—and after two children—we decided to stop being careful?

Henry and Anabel went with me to my first prenatal appointment. While waiting to see the doctor, Henry noticed the paper gown I was wearing. He began to poke at it and ripped it. Then Anabel started squealing and tore the gown off just as the doctor walked into the room to find me naked from the waist down.

He smiled and I uttered, "Do you think some women should stop at two?"

His response, "They're just kids being kids."

For the next seven months, his words, "They're just kids being kids," were replayed in my mind every time we went anywhere and wreaked havoc.

Baby Benjamin, was born in Ventura, California. He was our first colicky baby. Nine weeks after his birth, we moved to Portland, Oregon.

After a few months of madness, when our children seemed unhappy and the squabbling was unbearable, Jim and I went to a child psychologist to address sibling rivalry. The psychologist informed us that because we'd had our children so close together, they were not getting enough from me and were acting out for attention.

I left the appointment feeling sad, brooded for a minute with a chocolate chip cookie in my mouth, and then went to a park to prove that I could handle all three on the playground. I held Ben and pushed the older two on the swings. There was laughter and Ben smiled at the sight of his brother and sister soaring to the sky.

"We'll get through this. They'll be okay." I told myself.

It would have been the perfect afternoon if I hadn't locked my only set of keys in the car.

For Want of a Key
by Leesa Gehman

After the initial devastation over the end of my relationship with Tommy's father, I decided that I didn't need anyone. I could do this raising a kid thing perfectly fine on my own. I knew everything I needed to know (or I could read a book on it) and I didn't need anyone's help.

Teething questions? Scour the multitude of baby books I'd bought for answers. Don't like the sight of blood? Too bad, no queasiness allowed. Stomach virus? Can't immediately pass Tommy off to someone else and take a shower; instead it's a quick change and wipe down until the next projectile vomit. All I had to do was remember that I was strong, I was able to do this on my own, and I could handle anything that came my way by myself.

So, if I knew everything after a year of being a single mom, why had it never occurred to me to replace Tommy's bedroom doorknob with a lockless knob? That realization came when he was twenty-months old and hysterically crying in his bedroom. I was standing outside his room, completely befuddled by his brown door that, incomprehensibly, wouldn't open.

As he started to wail, I continued to jiggle the knob uselessly.

I tried to cajole him into turning the lock on the inside, but he'd already worked himself into hysteria and I didn't know if he'd understand the instructions anyway. So I searched the top of the doorframes for the straight piece of metal that acts like a key.

No dice. As he wailed in the background, I hunted for a bobby pin. However, I realized a few minutes into my quest that I long ago gave up fancy hairstyles for the ubiquitous ponytail. There was nary a bobby pin in the clutter of the bathroom. Another quick search, this time in the garage, finds that a flathead screwdriver and a Phillips are both too big for the hole.

Tommy's muffled wail was louder and was becoming frantic. He began slamming his little body against the door. I tried shouting words of comfort to him as I tore apart the house looking for anything that will open the stupid door.

In the cutlery drawer I found a meat thermometer. Hey, it was metal and thin. More importantly, it was the only thing I found in the entire house that would fit in the knob's hole. I inserted it, tried to find the magic spot and resulting click, but there was nothing. The lock didn't budge.

It really shouldn't have been that difficult to open a stupid door.

I went back to the screwdrivers. I used the flathead and took out two impossibly long screws from the knob. With a rattle, the outside handle fell into my hand and the inside one crashed onto the hardwood floor of his bedroom. The hole in the door was about three inches, with a metal frame webbing the inside. The solid metal lock was attached to the frame and then disappeared into the door. Using the screwdriver as a lever against the metal frame, I decided I could force out the lock.

Little fingers came scrambling through the hole, trying to reach me before I could attempt my lever maneuver. I cooed, told Tommy to move his fingers, placed the screwdriver into the metal frame and pushed.

The lock didn't move. Not a millimeter.

I tried again, using the screwdriver like a crowbar, throwing my body weight into it. Nothing.

"Damn it," I muttered. I've often said there are only two things I really need a man for: reaching stuff that's too high (so I don't have to get out a chair) and killing thousand-leggers. I decided my list might have to get bigger.

As it neared nine p.m., Tommy had been stuck in there close to an hour, and I was starting to feel as frantic as my kid. So I did what any reasonable person would. I swallowed my pride and called my mom. Who put my father on.

And conversations with my father can best be described as interesting.

"So wait—you tried to use a meat thermometer to unlock the door?"

"Yes, dad, I did, ok? It was the smallest and thinnest thing I could find in the house—you know, that's not the point. The point is it didn't work. I took the handle off when I couldn't get the meat thermometer to turn the mechanism in the lock."

"So the handle is off?"

"Yes."

"Can you get it back on? I think your best bet is to try it again."

"Dad. I can't get it back on. One side is on the floor in the hall. The other side is on the floor in his bedroom. Y'know, the bedroom he's locked in? And even if I could, I have a toddler trying to squeeze his entire body through a three-inch hole in the door. I can't explain to him how to put it back on." For a moment, I was reminded of childbirth.

There was a pause. "We'll be up in a few minutes."

Mom-Mom and Pop-Pop were there a quick fifteen minutes later and fifteen minutes after that my son was free. He hurled himself out of his room like he was on fire, tear-stained, sweaty, and hiccupping. His face was covered in snot. And as he wrapped his arms around me, the smell of poop wrapped around me, too. I covered him in kisses.

I think my mom might have told me once or twice (or fifty) times that my family would always be there to help me. But until I was holding Tommy my arms, both of us shaking with relief, I didn't really understand that what I thought was strength and resilience was really just pride and stubbornness. Sometimes it takes a tear-stained, poop-smelling twenty-month-old to show you that leaning on your family isn't necessarily weakness. It's just another part of mothering.

I just wish I had known that before Tommy locked himself

in a bedroom and scared the bejesus out of both of us. But I'm grateful that was the worst that happened.

The next day, I put the knob back on with the lock on the outside. I bought a flat key for the interior doors (and some bobby pins, just in case). I tried to make sure my son knew how to turn the lock on the knob, which didn't really work, but made me feel better anyway. I tickled him, laughed with him, and covered him with kisses. And I wondered if he'd lock himself in the bathroom next.

At least I have a key. But more importantly, I have my parents on speed dial.

Raising the Enemy
by Suzanne Jurva

Being a mom to two teenagers is like living in a triage unit and performing battlefield medicine. In triage, the situation is divided into three groups:

1. Those who will not make it.
2. Those who will make it without medical intervention.
3. Those who need medical attention immediately to survive.

Moms of teenagers make those psychological choices continuously–most often landing on number 3. Emergencies pop up like a new zit on the most important day of your life (to use a teenage metaphor) and have to be popped and covered immediately.

Situations arise, such as an overheard conversation that the Coach wants your kid off the team, which demand immediate intervention. Instead, you get that sinking feeling in your stomach, realizing that there is nothing you ever said or did to prepare your child for this.

We are commanders of a ship with a wobbly steering wheel. Our hands are on the wheel, but the turns are not the ones we intended. The sole soldier in the foxhole summoned only when our teenager needs money or a ride somewhere.

The daily battles wear me out, not just with my kids, who are not bad teenagers, but with outside people. The small circle becomes larger and larger with each new school, sport, club, musical instrument, friend, text message, cell phone call, and Face Book entry. My daily encounters include people I cannot relate to and would never choose to have a conversation with. Now I must deal with them as I am enlisted in this phase of parenthood. Let me tell you it is nasty in battlefield suburbia.

But just when the hostility is too overwhelming and I con-template taking the poison pill, something sweet happens. Yesterday, my son celebrated his thirteenth birthday. He didn't want anything fancy or costly, just the most important thing in his life—food. So the four of us had a quiet, simple dinner including his favorite macaroni and cheese, chocolate cake and ice cream. It was actually fun; he loved his wave-rider skate-board, and gave me a hug. No arguing with his sister, no com-plaining, no nothing.

Those moments allow a mom of a teenager to go on—to pitch the tent, get out the supplies, and say to the world, "Throw anything at me, I am armed and ready."

Notes from the Bathroom Floor
by Leigh Kaufman Leveen

Last night, my family was sick—I mean the vomiting, diarrhea kind that infiltrates the whole clan. My one year old got it a few days ago, and last night she was more management than crisis, while my 5 year-old paid direct homage to the porcelain god, with my husband occupying the other bathroom in the same position. I can only think it was the mother of mothers who was looking out for me by not allowing me to get sick. Oh, if I had been sick, I would have crawled out of bed and taken the best care I could. It is what I have learned is required in motherhood—a devotion, a commitment, a life-long pursuit that cannot be compared to any other relationship.

Sometimes, I think that it is all too much, too overwhelming, too enormous, this trust that is laid on me to carry out the raising of a child. I did not know how to do so many simple things—like change a diaper on a wiggly infant—when I first became a parent. The books had not prepared me for the wide range of emotions I would feel, and if there were a chapter on handling the kind of volcanic upset I often felt, well, I was usually too upset to figure out what chapter I could find it in.

Sitting on the bathroom floor, stroking my son's back, twinges of pink in the morning sky had arrived. As I closed my eyes from blistering fatigue, I thought through the rest of the morning. My son would hopefully transfer to his own bed and I could go make some industrial grade caffeine. My daughter would need breakfast. My husband said he needed Gatorade, so I will run to the pharmacy. Gatorade, Pedialyte, anything else that will tide them over. As I run through all of this in a matter of seconds, I hold fast to the image of the candy rows near the cash register. Usually, I rant at such placement of sugar, as typical marketing excursions end as I throw candy bars out of the shopping cart as fast as the little ones throw them back in—some game. But this morning, I wanted, no, I needed, something I shouldn't have, something that said "reward." I scanned the rows mentally and settled on the orange and yellow wrapper of a Reese's. The peanut butter center came alive for me as I imagined how delectable it would taste.

I heard all the hype during pregnancy about getting my sleep while I could, and going to the movies before it became a $100 excursion, what with a sitter, tickets, parking, and a tub of popcorn to satiate the need to vacuum in calories just to stay awake for that dud of a flick. And then when you get home you will find a screaming child who only goes to sleep when you do it just the right way.

I heard this and thought, "That won't be me! I'm different; those women can't possibly have a clue. I can multi-task, and my husband will free me up to take care of myself when I need it." Hmm. What I have learned is that parenthood is a 24/7 job, which means all the time. It means when you are trying to sleep, it means when you are sick and so are they, it means all those inconvenient times when you just need a break. You are always a mother. You never get a vacation; you never get to stop worrying about your child.

As the sun grew brighter, the bathroom moved from grey to pink to white light. Lying on the cold bathroom floor was not the quality time people talk about spending with your child, but it is crucial. And I see how quickly it all passes. Time shift shapes when you enter motherhood. I used to count time in chunks of sleep. Now, I count time in length of school days, and vacation periods. I count how many play-dates I can fit into a weekend, and I count how many days overdue I am at Blockbuster. I know that I am preparing for the day when he starts counting his own time, as in how much more time he can he spend out on a Saturday night.

But I am not complaining—I would not trade this life. Those hours spent by my son's side in the bathroom are part of the job description. I leapt out of bed when I heard him crying for me. He needed me and I was there for him. His trust in me was unconditional and his love still pure. Motherhood is full of these simple, yet heart-stopping moments. They sneak up on you and leave you wanting more.

Dear Mom-to-be:
Angela Sandelier

I f you only knew the truth about what you were in for, you'd run for your life. Colic, anyone? How about endless ear infections, a messy house, alienation from the outside world, physical exhaustion, sleep deprivation, zero sex drive and loss of privacy and freedom? Not to mention lack of disposable income (since it's all being spent on disposable diapers), traveling the world or finishing up that degree, at least for now.

What can I tell you that will make your path to motherhood a bit easier? Pull up a chair, girlfriend, you're about to find out.

* Drop the guilt. You can love your children and not love the actual process of raising them. It does not make you a bad mother to hate poopy diapers, and vomit at 2 a.m.

* Don't sweat the small stuff. Diapers, pacifiers, and baby food addictions will eventually disappear. No one ever showed up in kindergarten eating Gerber Stage 2. Biters will eventually learn to talk. Hitters will learn that "hands are not for hitting."

* You won't ever qualify as the "perfect" mom, so don't let the pursuit of perfection overshadow moments of pure joy.

* Put yourself on the "to do list." Get a regular pedicure, massage, or time-out with your girlfriends.

* Embrace the minivan instead of the Jeep; the Mom jeans instead of suits and high heels.

* Learn to love your face without make up, your body with all of its new curves.

* Realize that you will regain your libido and your mind eventually (even if you think it has been turned to mush by Candy Land marathons). You will regain your sense of self.

So how will you survive motherhood, the toughest job you'll ever love? Trust your instincts.

And eat chocolate—lots and lots of chocolate. A glass of wine never hurt anyone either.

From a mom in the trenches,
Angela Sandelier

Chapter 2:

Mother May I?

Fertilizer
by Cynthia Jenkins

W hat I looked forward to most about being a mom were the big earrings and jingly bracelets. Oh, and the meat loafs, too. Because all moms are great cooks, right? And I should know because I grew up with the best.

And you guessed it, with big earrings and jingly bracelets.

"When does that woman ever sleep?" my friend's mom would ask. I suppose as a divorced, working mother of three, the answer was probably never. But that didn't stop her from indulging our 'no-crust', 'yes-crust' and 'I-don't-care-as-long-it's-cut-in-triangles' sack lunches. Nor did it keep her from our carpools, retainer replacements, or any of our three-hour plays during which we each played the same mute tree.

Everyone tells us we look identical. Our eyes are the same blue; our blond comes from the same bottle, so undoubtedly her mom shoes should fit me just right too. Except that I'm a terrible cook. In fact, someone once told me my meatloaf tastes "a little like fertilizer." And the jingle of those bracelets? They drive me crazy by my second cup of coffee. So I looked for other signs of maternal transformation as I gazed into my firstborn's eyes. A wisp of my mother's hair, the unmistakable scent of Chloe, anything linking me to the matriarchal throne I now shared. But all I saw was me. A freckly-faced, TV-watching thirty-something has-been with a cell phone perpetually stuck to her ear. Who could make a mean fertilizer.

"When you get hungry, I'll fly down and make you a meat loaf, honey," my mom advised. "Just be yourself."

But who was I? And what was natural for me? I knew that I never laughed at kids in high school when they'd trip and fall. In fact, I'd even help them—regardless of their status. And I'd always remember subordinates' birthdays at the office—we'd start celebrating early even, making it their "birthday week!" And if a pal has spinach stuck in her teeth, of course I'd tell her. Geez, I'd tell a stranger if I got close enough!

So, you know, I'm pretty thoughtful.

But does that make me a mom?

Well, how about watching every single E! True Hollywood Story ever made? Or the ability to finagle my son into a Bjorn single-handedly while balancing a glass of wine in the other?

Does that make it so?

Well, the answer is yes. Precisely what I wish I had known before becoming a mom. Because the moment that baby is plucked out of the vessel you once called your body, you become, well, still you.

You smell the same, you kiss the same, and you make the same fertilizer. Your husband's jokes? Still not funny. Your hairdresser's love life? Still picking the wrong guy. And the ability to become lost for hours in front of a blank screen is still there. Except now you're staring at your sleeping kids' faces, stroking their hair, folding and unfolding their teeny fingers, longing for their endless lashes. But come morning, your same socks peel out of the same bed, they pit-pat to the same refrigerator, and they tip-toe to reach the same brand of coffee grounds you've drunk since you-don't-know-when.

While this may seem depressing, think about the alternative. What if you actually did have to become someone else the moment you became a mom? Your private parts are fried, your breasts are blistered, your eyes need to be held open with toothpicks and, KAZAM! Not only do you need to care for a newborn, but you're forced to become someone you've never met. A mirage of a mom you strive to emulate if only she would sit still for just one minute. Which, of course, is impossible. Because (as my mother revealed while she confessed her meatloaf was store-bought), she was never in the room to begin with.

This epiphany provided great comfort to me as I braced myself for a second child. In fact, while preparing for a natural childbirth at a yoga class, (failing, I might add. Once a pill-popper, always a pill-popper as this theory goes) the yogi announced that we "all are the perfect parents for our children, just as we are." She actually said this, and looked directly at me. I wanted to call out that while I appreciated her optimism, she should know that I'm a disaster in the kitchen and that noisy jewelry completely unnerves me. But, alas, the yoga breathing left me breathless, swallowing my confession before it had a chance. So I held onto that "mantra," if you will. And I do to this day.

So when my kids fall, I pick them up as I've always done. And their birthdays? They last least a week, too. (The spinach-in the-teeth thing I'm still working on, though—I'm usually too distracted by the fact I got a vegetable down them to say much.)

What I finally learned about becoming a mother after becoming a mother was that I'm not my mother. I am just me—an offense to all things culinary and jingly. But I'm also a mom who understands the importance of her kids being themselves, too. Which is precisely the role of a good fertilizer, isn't it? To help things grow.

Comanche Child
by Elaine Greensmith Jordan

"Mom! The adoption searcher just called. They've found my birth family!" My daughter's voice over the telephone from central Oregon sounded thick with urgent joy. "I couldn't even talk to the lady," she went on. "I started crying. I can't believe it!"

"That's wonderful," I said, meaning it.

We'd been searching for Caroline's birth family for ten years and had never broken through the barriers of secrecy. I'd spent over four thousand dollars paying the expenses of detectives, Internet geniuses, and outright scammers. Then one day Caroline's aching stomach made her angry about not knowing her health history. Did her birth family have colon problems, or cancer? She and her two daughters had a right to know. She went to a website, gave her credit card number, and paid for another searcher she'd learned of on the television show, "Montel," I think it's called.

"They live in Oklahoma on the Comanche Reservation," Caroline went on, and I could hear her fighting tears. "I guess I'm a real Indian. My other mother works in a smoke shop.

Isn't that funny?"

"Doesn't matter. It's just wonderful. Smoke shop?"

"I think the searcher must've called everyone on the reservation. I'm so scared. Wish you were here." She started to cry.

"I know, honey," I said. I could picture my daughter on her back patio, a green lawn and vegetable garden extending out from the small cement pad. She'd be holding her cell phone, a cigarette in the other hand, tears streaming. "I've never been to Oklahoma," I added. "I picture tornados. Comanche are plains' Indians, I think, and they're expert riders. You've always loved horses."

"All I can think of is 'Dancing with Wolves,'" she said, her voice in a higher register. "Mom, she's almost got my name—Carley. I wonder if I could join the tribe. I mainly want to know where I came from. I think they've a college there—maybe my kids could go. I'm so excited," she said, panting. "Sometimes I forget to breathe."

"It would be fun to give your kids Indian names."

"Yeah," she said, coughing. "I think I'd call my Sara, 'Runs with No Shoes.'"

I turned to look outdoors at the wind-tossed flowers on our deck. Though I live in northern Arizona, those few pansies and petunias evoke the colors of San Diego I'd always miss. Perhaps my daughter's spirit craved an Oklahoma landscape in the same way I yearned for California and the flowers of San Diego.

You might wonder why I'd tried so hard to help out

on this search for a birth mother. Caroline had been a cranky sullen youngster who fought with her brother and the neighbors' children. Then my wild child became an angry teen. I was a divorced single mom, and my daughter was my nemesis. Frankly, she'd brought so much chaos into my life that I was eager back then to help her find someone else, a ghost mother, to answer her needs. At the lowest points, I wished she were not in my life.

"Mom," Caroline said the next day, after she'd talked at length over the telephone with her birth mother, "this is pretty funny. Carley's done time; she's got tattoos like mine, and she's a biker."

"Does that upset you?" I asked, knowing I looked like a bespectacled librarian.

"Not really." She paused. "Carley seems nice, and she wants to see me. Besides, I was pretty wild myself." Caroline had, indeed, 'done time.' She'd been a year in juvenile lock-up and had endured months of drug rehab when she was a teenager. "It's so great not to be lost any more. Did you know I'm related to Jim Thorpe? I looked him up on the Internet. Cool."

"I've been waiting so long for you to claim your Indian heritage," I said. "I'm excited too."

"I know," she said. "You kept putting Indian stuff around and trying to get me interested. Now I'm really interested. Carley says I have two brothers. Oh Mom, two brothers! Maybe they look like me." Caroline paused as if absorbing a universe of images.

Thoughts of Native American faces brought back my memories of walking the late-night streets looking for Caroline. On my walks I nurtured my fantasy about Caroline's Native American birth mother. This ghost mother of my imagination would have the wisdom of an Indian matriarch—the kind who gazes in solemn profile at the mountains—and would offer my daughter unconditional love. I longed for another mother who would know how to discipline Caroline, how to lift the sadness that seemed to linger around her mouth. I knew the real Carley wasn't my fantasy Indian woman, but she was a person you could look at and talk to. I sensed that's what my daughter needed now.

"Son-au-uuat," Caroline said. "That's my birth grandmother's name. I'm going to find out what it means."

I don't know if that name translates or if I could pronounce it. It resounds with the unfamiliar, untold stories of cultures lost, of deep urges for identity. I do know that with a living birth mother and family, Caroline can now fill the "hole in her heart," as some have phrased the feeling of not knowing their origins. She says she felt lost, and I can't think of anything sadder. I used to have dreams of being lost, unable to find my way home.

I've read that our children are not ours to own but are like arrows we send out from us. That image fits my Native American daughter well. A month after that first telephone call, Caroline left her Oregon home, taking her husband and daughters to meet her Comanche tribe and her two half-brothers.

She sailed—as if shot from a taut bow—to Oklahoma and came back with a calmer stomach and a landscape as firmly fixed in her heart as California is in mine.

Rough Cut
by Barbara Eknoian

I f I'd seen the rushes,
I would have known
sometimes a child
needs more than a caring parent,
needs a strong mother,
guiding him from a director's chair,
megaphone in hand,
shouting,
"Stand over there.
Now, strut down the street
like John Travolta with a cocky grin,
hear the music beat within your being.
Don't stand on the sidelines,
step to center stage,
never mind the Oscar,
enjoy the process
as you star
in the film
of your life."

Mom Without A Safety Net
by Mary Anne O'Connell

"You're going to make a great mom." "Your pelvis was built to have babies." "Having a child will make you so happy."

These were the words I heard before getting pregnant that were meant to quiet any uncertainties lying in the back of my mind about having a baby. But how did people know I would be a great mom? Was the gynecologist really able to tell I was built to have babies just because I kept losing diaphragms up the 'ol birth canal? And what if my dream of becoming a mom someday came true and I was not happy?

The excitement over the fact that our baby was conceived on Groundhog's Day slowly disappeared, as my tummy grew larger. The closer the due date came, the more I began to think about my future and my past. My mother died right after I turned 12 years old. I never had a sister, an aunt, or grandmother. Any role models who entered my life after my mother died were few and far between.

My journey into adolescence and adulthood was very difficult, how I made it out alive is still a mystery. But here I was with a husband, a baby on the way, and all I could think about was how in the world was I going to pull this off? Now is the time when a girl needs her mother and I didn't have one. How would I know what to do? Does this stuff come naturally? My mom had not been around long enough to teach me how to be a mother.

My first child was two-weeks overdue, so I was admitted into the hospital for an induced labor. Before beginning the Pitocin drip, one final ultrasound was done and guess what? My baby was breech. I was sent home and a C-section was scheduled for later that week. Not only did this news scare the heck out of me, but I also could not help feeling I had somehow failed. I wanted to experience "real" childbirth—the pain, the pushing, and the pain. It just wasn't going to happen, so I tucked those feelings away.

My baby girl was beautiful, ten fingers and ten toes. Why then was I not beaming with happiness? I thought everyone said having a baby was supposed to make me happy. My emotions (and hormones) were all over the place, and my insecurities about being a mom were rearing their ugly heads. Here I was holding my dream and I just didn't feel the connection. What was wrong with me?

At first I wanted to blame my mother, she had to be the reason I was emotionally frozen. But after shedding lots of tears, hours of researching on the Internet, and a few office visits with the pediatrician, I learned what I was feeling wasn't that abnormal. More importantly, it wasn't my mother's fault. Sometimes the "mother-baby bond" happens immediately and sometimes it takes longer.

Days turned into weeks. I spent hours just holding her, looking into her eyes and watching her sleep. Before long, this amazing feeling came over me. I could not imagine life without her. She became part of me and I became part of her.

After a few years, Baby No. 2 came along and, guess what? I got to experience a real birth. Yeah! As time passed, I couldn't help but feel like I was getting the hang of this Mom-thing. I was really doing it. Our little family of four was thriving and growing, and I was having a blast.

Even though my mother's presence in my life was short, it hit me one day that she had been a good role model. She had shown me how to love. I recalled watching her interact with friends and neighbors. She had truly loved everyone unconditionally, no strings attached, no agenda, she just cared. I don't think there was one selfish bone in her body.

I realized that it's not the length of time you have role models, but the lessons they teach you.

What I Know Now
by Geri Jacobs

A new world opens by simply becoming a mom. Life with children teaches us many valuable lessons in humility, understanding and decision-making that cannot be learned from other people's experiences.

The road is not always smooth; it has bumps, hairpin curves and alternate routes.

We indulge our children for the satisfaction and pleasure of seeing them smile.

We hold our breath as they ski the slopes or drive a car for the first time—the same breath we held as they took their first steps.

The thrill of a kindergarten graduation equals the thrill of a college graduation.

Our hopes are realized in their achievement and happiness.

We have dreams for our children, but accept the fact that their dreams might not reflect ours.

Nothing can be changed, everything has to be accepted and our children will have the same opportunity to learn from their own experiences.

The best dividends of being a parent are having grandchildren who view you in the same innocent, trusting, loving way that your children did.

The surprises, adventures and fun are still exciting and all the pleasures and the smiles and the tears and the cheers have a second chance for renewal.

Life would be boring if we knew in advance what the future will bring. Looking back puts the parenting experience into perspective.

Veteran Mom
by Mary Helen Berg

No one told me that having children would mean spending sixteen years in elementary school. I always thought my children would be close enough in age that they could be pals and schoolmates. Instead, my kids are so far apart, my friends think I failed a course in family planning. At school, students graduate, teachers retire, the administration changes and I am still reading Dr. Seuss in the first grade. I suppose I can provide institutional memory for the school before I am institutionalized myself.

My three kids are in high school, middle school and early elementary school. This age spread is an eternity to most of my friends.

"What were you thinking?" they say with a snicker. It's true that our youngest looks like the proverbial "accident." She's five years behind her brother and I was nearly 40 when she was born, but truly, we had her as soon as we caught our breath after our second child.

Still, I understand why those friends laugh at us. They know there are tricky things about the age range, and it would have been easier if we had quit before the third child. At our house, there is little that interests everyone at once. We can't all play Scrabble or see the same movie. One wants the playground while the other plans an evening at a nightclub. My teenager announced her first boyfriend while the youngest found her first loose tooth. The boy in the middle holds his own against waves of dress-up and make-up.

Then there is the thorough exhaustion that somehow appeared in the years between children. Let's face it; we don't run around the playground as we once did. We watch.

There is also something a little lonely about having a third child after our friends are long finished building their families. Her late arrival means I am still attending play dates and field trips to the pumpkin patch while many of my friends are beginning second careers, seeking master's degrees, moving on. Part of me feels left behind.

Friends I haven't seen in awhile always ask: "Are you writing?" They figure I've been mothering for 15 years already, I must have had time to write. The truth is, I haven't written much. I've been a school board trustee, a soccer coach, a chauffeur, a social organizer, a fundraiser, a chauffeur, a family historian and photographer, a chauffeur, accountant, general contractor, and a chauffeur, but no, haven't written much. Every year I think: "This is the year I start to write" and every year I'm wrong.

Meanwhile the parents of my children's friends keep getting younger—and groovier. I am Veteran Mom. I nod politely while they fret over whether Susie will read and gossip about who didn't get invited to which birthday. The first time around, I was in the thick of these conversations, now I find that I try not to offer unsolicited advice for fear of sounding like an old warhorse.

I already have my own answers to frequently asked questions: What do you do about allowance? (One dollar per week per grade. With monetary gifts, have your children divide the money in three: one third to save, one third for charity and one third to spend as they like.) What do you tell your 5-year-old when he or she asks about sex? (Answer them honestly, but keep details to a minimum. You know they have heard enough when they cover their ears and say: "Yuck.")

How old is your oldest? these newer parents ask. Wow, they say, awestruck, as if they can't believe I have survived the intervening years.

Don't get me wrong; there are benefits to having children so far apart. The oldest can baby-sit for the youngest. In fact, she can pay for college by babysitting for her little sister's friends. Maybe when she gets her license she can be the new chauffeur and drive her sister to ballet, soccer, and play dates. The oldest has already predicted that I will buy her a car.

"Why in the world would I do that?" I asked her.

"Because, you hate to drive us around." Come to think of it, maybe she can drive to the grocery store, too.

I know that deep down, my friends, mothers of teenagers, felt pangs of jealousy when I announced I was pregnant with that third baby. Although a new baby in any of their lives would have thrown them (not to mention we were all on the verge of too old), a baby is a promise and they all remember the miraculous tiny weight of a new one in their arms. The memory of new baby smell rendered some of them temporarily insane enough to venture discussions with their husbands. The husbands told them to snap out of it.

Now that my third baby is (finally) school age, my friends laugh with pity at the idea that I must slog again through the same demanding elementary school rituals; the same fundraisers and field trips and friendship dramas. The same politics with younger faces attached. I groan and go along. But I think I still sense their envy, wistfulness for a time that passed too quickly.

After all, we are at a stage where our parents are ill and best friends are divorcing or even dying young and the simplicity of the playground is something to long for. As my friends' teen children push them away, I still have a small hand that actually seeks mine and then holds it like she will never let go. So, although some days it seem as if I will never graduate from elementary school, that little hand keeps me warm and reminds me that it was totally worth sitting through kindergarten orientation—yet again. I guess if all we ever need to know we learn in kindergarten, then I am very well educated indeed.

Chapter 3:

Feeding the Zoo

Motherhood: It's a Man's Job
by Frank Leggett

When my wife and I decided that I would become a Home Dad and she would return to work—effectively making me Mom—I had no idea what I was doing. I figured that running the house and raising the kids couldn't possibly take more than a couple of hours a day. In my imagination I saw myself tucking my exhausted little darlings into bed after a fun-filled day full of imaginative play, unconscious learning and military-style order. With all my spare time I could probably write that novel I had been thinking about for so long.

I know, I know. I had a lot to learn about being a parent and even more to learn about being a mom. Here are my revelations.

1. All children are liars.
You heard me. Barefaced, unrepentant, remorseless liars. They are as incorrigible as a room full of Enron executives. I once had reason to ask my 3-year-old daughter, "Did you eat that chocolate?" She shook her head and looked at me with such guilt-free innocence that I almost believed her.

Except, of course, for her chocolate-smeared face, cheeks bulging with ill-gotten booty and the torn wrapper still grasped in her hot little hand. Being caught in the act means nothing to children. They simply deny, deny, deny! Surely such criminal tendencies can't be in the genes.

2. Children have an exquisite sense of timing.

Every time I ask the question, "Do you need to go to the toilet?" the answer is always, "No, Daddy." "Are you sure?" "Yes, Daddy." "Let's sit you on the toilet." Ten minutes later, "Nothing, Daddy, I can't go." So, foolishly forgetting Point 1, I load up the kids, go to the supermarket and fill my trolley to the brim. At that moment a little hand pulls on my shirt and a serious little face informs me, "Gotta do poo, Daddy." The line at each checkout is conservatively two miles long. "Can you hold it?" "No, Daddy." So I pick up one child, drag the other one behind me and run through the mall searching for one of those bathrooms they hide down the end of camouflaged corridors. "Hurry Daddy, it's starting to come." Of course, when I return to the supermarket some helpful clerk has unloaded my trolley so I buy a couple of frozen pizzas and that's dinner. Stuck in a traffic jam on the way home my other child then says, "Gotta do a wee, Dad."

3. Housework is not done by the cleaning pixies.

Do you know that once you clean something it doesn't stay clean?! I have discovered that I can vacuum a room and it may need to be vacuumed AGAIN as soon as six weeks later. It's the same with mopping floors. And clothes washing never stops! I mean it! The laundry basket is never empty. I have been a Home Dad now for three years and still haven't seen the bottom of the basket. There must be clothes down there, quietly moldering away, that are now sadly out of fashion. And one last thing—whoever invented the dishwasher should be made a Saint. Forget penicillin, walking on the moon and creating fire—the dishwasher is the pinnacle of humankind's achievement.

4. What you don't see can't hurt you.

This is my official Home Dad cleaning motto. That crumpet stuck down the side of the oven, those toys jammed under the couch, that drift of dust under the bed is of no matter because in my house, out of sight is out of mind.

5. After school activities will always be on the same day and as far away from each other as possible.

This is simply an unalterable fact of life. If you live in Kansas, your son's baseball practice will be in Venice Beach and your daughter's ballet lessons will be in Manhattan and you will have 20 minutes to drive from one to the other.

6. Children can live on a very limited diet.

My eldest son has just completed his first year of school and has had the same lunch every day for the entire year. Any attempt to change or widen this selection was met with a stubborn refusal to eat. Initially, I had visions of nothing but fresh, healthy, organic food passing my children's lips. Two weeks after adopting the mantle of Home Dad I was happy if they ate half a PB & J. I once served steamed fish fillets, broccolini, mashed potato and organic tomato slices drizzled with virgin olive oil. By their reaction, anyone would have thought I was serving cat food. Their favorite meal is tuna pasta. Here's how you cook it. One: Boil some pasta. Two: Upend a can of tuna on it. Three: Serve.

7. It only hurts if you can see it.

If one of my kids gets the smallest scrape, they react as if they are being dismembered with a rusty knife. If they spy a spot of blood, people three suburbs away are made aware of it. However, apply that miracle of anesthesiology—a small plastic band-aid—and the pain magically dissipates and it's back to the playground again.

8. The three sweetest words in the English language are not "I love you."

Not by a long shot. "They are asleep" comes close. "Here's the babysitter" is in the running. But the loveliest of all is to look at the calendar and see "School Holidays end."

Not much for three years of full-time child rearing, I admit. And yet, as I sit here in my moderately clean home amongst the piles of moderately clean laundry with my moderately serious drinking problem (joking! sort of) I recall those times that make it all worthwhile. My daughter's happy smile when I pick her up from pre-school. My son's unbridled joy at riding a bike without trainer wheels for the first time. I was there for those occasions when the vast majority of fathers were stuck at work.

So, what do I know now that I didn't know before becoming a parent? Well, as I have virtually no memory of the time before I was a parent, that's an impossible question to answer. I will say this, though— being a mom, even if you're a dad, is the best job in the world.

How to Get Your Children to Behave in 5, ~~10~~, ~~13~~, 435 Easy Steps
by Pat Dunnigan

My friends are always asking me to share my best techniques for getting children to behave, to cooperate and to help around the house in an agreeable manner. For a long time, I imagined this was an area of parenting in which I was considered an authority. I was happy to share my tips.

But slowly I came to realize that these requests always seemed to come at cocktail parties or other social gatherings. No one ever asked me for advice over the telephone.

I was a source of entertainment, not expertise. I was doing stand-up and I didn't even know it.

So go ahead and laugh at my coffee cans, my little slips of paper, my constantly evolving systems of points, check marks and gold stars, the privileges bestowed and revoked, the statements of principles taped to the refrigerator, entire justice systems erected and scrapped over a period of days.

Here is an example of the kind of parenting creativity that will eventually earn me a patent and then who will be laughing?

New Improved Parenting System for Ending Epidemics of Constant Bickering, Sibling Spats and All Around Lack of Cooperation

Materials Needed:

1. One empty coffee can
2. One pad of multicolored Post-It notes.
   (Buttons, coins or other tokens can be substituted)
3. Paper to label coffee can
4. List of chores or good behaviors that can be used to earn points
5. List of privileges or treats that can be earned by performing chores or exhibiting good behaviors
6. Independent, outside auditor (recommended)

Procedures:

1. Adopt an accounting system that reflects the relationship (in points, stars or tokens) between behaviors or chores you wish to be exhibited/accomplished and various treats and/or privileges to be used as incentives.
2. Adopt a separate accounting system that reflects a subtraction of credit for failure to exhibit certain behaviors or complete assigned chores.
3. Keep track of good behaviors exhibited/chores accomplished by dropping a token or post-it note into the can whenever necessary.

4. Keep track of failure to exhibit certain behavior or complete assigned chores by withdrawing points, tokens or stars from coffee can.

5. Allow child to redeem points by choosing from list of treats/privileges.

I felt certain that this is a system that could work eventually, despite the setbacks we experienced.

It started out fine. My One Cooperative Child (a.k.a. "the suck-up") was ready to give it a go. Then came the 12-year-old: a boy who could talk a second-year law student out of his position, whose recall of precedents would get him past the bar exam in most states and who can spot the loopholes in new household legislation before the glue is dry on the coffee can.

We call him Boy Esquire.

Boy, Esq.: I have a question.

Mommy: Yes?

Boy, Esq.: Does "trip to bookstore" mean we get to buy a book? Any book? Does it have to be a book?

We settled upon a reasonable system for determining what kind of purchases could be made during a bookstore reward trip and 45 minutes later, we were ready to restart.

Then: Boy Esq.: When do we get to go to the bookstore? Whenever we want? Because what would be the point if we had to wait until you wanted to go to the bookstore? We get to do that already.

A lengthy discussion followed wherein we settled this issue

and numerous others. Could points be borrowed or traded? What if one child had enough for a trip to the bookstore but the other didn't and couldn't be left behind? Also, would the accounting system use negative numbers?

But what really killed the system was my failure to develop a corresponding system of appeals.

Boy, Esq. hit upon this after a discussion of whether or not credit could be earned or subtracted for chores or behaviors not explicitly enumerated on the can.

As the creator and arbiter of the system, I felt that I should be free to consider other behaviors.

Boy Esq. was willing to stipulate to this, but was troubled by the system's lack of appellate procedure. Could protests be lodged?

In a flash of brilliance, I decided to include "arguing about the system" as a two-point offense.

This was a critical improvement, despite the obvious equal protection implications.

But by the end of the first day in conference committee, we had developed more amendments than would fit on the outside of the can. So we decided to scrap the can and go to the notebook system.

The notebook was plagued by "self-accounting" and some outright forgery. At the moment, I cannot say exactly where it is.

Thank you. You've been a wonderful audience. I will be here all week.

Caution: Warning Label Not Included
by Jennifer A. Davis

Warning: Having a child will drastically change your life. Each child is unique and may not be what you pictured or expected. If you are not completely satisfied with your child, you cannot send him back or return her. Motherhood is not for the fainthearted. Please be advised of the following:

✳ When your child falls asleep in the car, keep the car moving. If you have to drop something off at a friend's house, call ahead and have your friend meet you outside. When you pull up to her house, slow down to about five miles per hour, roll down the window, and toss the item to your friend. This is known as the "mommy drive by."

✳ Changing an infant's diaper requires great skill. You must be prepared to do it as quickly as possible. The second you lift up the infant's legs to wipe its bottom, poop is bound to come shooting out. If you have a boy, you have a double whammy, so watch out for shooting pee.

✳ Just when you think you are done with diapers you realize that potty training is much harder. One common training technique is to put Cheerios in the toilet and tell your child to aim at them. Unfortunately, this can backfire if you drop a Cheerio on the ground. Should this happen, cover your head immediately. It is probably your little boy taking a wiz over the banister aiming at the dropped Cheerio below. Remember, you can't yell at him because you are trying to encourage him not to pee in his diaper.

✳ Children are like time bombs that can explode at any minute. When your child asks for something to drink, it means apple juice in the pink cup with two ice cubes and the liquid level at the halfway point. Anything else will cause an explosion.

✳ Instead of fighting over who has to clean up after dinner, you will actually fight over who *gets* to clean up after dinner. The person who is lucky enough to do the dishes has a break from the children while the other one has to start giving baths. Washing dishes can be quite peaceful.

✳ Throwing up always happens at night, when the child is in bed, and you are (were) in a deep sleep.

Raising a child is WORK but there isn't another job I would rather have. The days are long but the years are short.

Enjoy it while you can.

Becoming Mom
by Regina Nervo

That the oatmeal would never be sweet enough.
That there would never be enough milk.

That I can't save the lunch stained shirt.
That the butterfly would not hatch.

That I can't stop the budding of breasts.
That I can't untangle a Mobius strip.
or change an animal's behavior.

That we are no longer Venus and Adonis
but Ray and Debra stuck in a sitcom.

That I would find solace and be preoccupied.
That there is no coaching allowed from the sidelines.

That my children would travel and return
with handfuls of sand and declare
to me their pure love grain by grain.

Bad Mother, Bad Woman
by Peggy Rambach

I am a bad mother.

I realized this, years ago, when my younger daughter requested Doritos for breakfast and I refused to give it to her. In the following half hour, she demanded in at least sixteen different ways that I justify this decision. And I attempted at least sixteen different explanations that degenerated from a clear description of Doritos' nutritional value to: "Because it's a disgusting thing to eat for breakfast!" delivered in a raised voice.

This is something good mothers do not do. They do not raise their voices, slam doors, hit car steering wheels, use offensive language, leave marriages, cry from heartbreak, frustration, fatigue and from watching a good kiss on a TV drama. They do not play rock 'n' roll loud enough to cause their children to order them to turn it down. They have about as much sexuality as Mother Bear of the Berenstain Bear Series, do not panic over the Morning Poofy Hair Syndrome, and most of all, they ask nothing for themselves. They sacrifice, sacrifice, sacrifice.

What, exactly, good mothers sacrifice is never very clear. My guess is things they do by themselves and for themselves.

The reason I know this is that I was once a good mother, and a good wife, and a good employee. Yes, it's true. I'd tried my best in all these roles to be placid, tolerant, compliant, and above all, selfless and self-sacrificing. I behaved the way women still think they should behave to be considered, well, good. So regardless of whether a woman is or is not a mother, if she does not behave like a good one, she is bad.

I guess, then, that's me. Bad mother. Bad woman. I have a temper and I lose it. I look (tastefully, I hope) like I do do the thing and enjoy doing the thing that made my children in the first place. And I consider my own growth and aspirations to be equal in value to those of the people I love. And if these people are healthy, I ask of them, no—demand of them, the same degree of sacrifice for my needs that I am willing to give theirs.

My daughters were on to me. Along with their own aspirations, they intended to play keyboard and lead guitar in my future rock band. My older daughter wanted to create and direct my music videos. And eventually, the younger one learned to wait patiently for me to finish my before-breakfast writing-time, to suggest that we compromise on Gummy Bears.

Because they knew, and still know, now in their early twenties, that to ask for something for themselves does not make them selfish, does not make them bad women, and will not make them bad mothers because the more fulfilled they are the better they will love.

So I guess my daughters turned out pretty bad too, which is good.

Do It Yourself
by Gloria Zimmerman

I recently read an article about a well-known politician whose wife expects their 6 and 9-year old children to set their own alarm clocks every night. Instilling this kind of self-reliance in our 7-year-old twins is an idea that my husband and I also greatly value. Puzzling then, to find myself most mornings pretending to be a bear, sniffing at my daughter to nudge her awake while she plays dead. Meanwhile, in the kitchen, my husband methodically spoon-feeds our son his breakfast cereal. No worries, though, if neither child manages to eat the most important meal of the day before we leave for school. My car is a virtual 7-11 on wheels with an impressive array of beverages and snacks. They won't go hungry.

It's difficult to imagine my own mother going to such lengths to make sure I ate. Once the food hit the table, her job was done. If I didn't like what was on the menu, so what? There wasn't a lot of coddling in my house. I had a long list of much-resented responsibilities, but maybe it was intended to prod me toward self-reliance.

Here is an abbreviated list of my household chores growing up: vacuuming the house from top to bottom every other weekend, doing my laundry and scheduling all my own doctor appointments. I distinctly remember walking to the dentist's office by myself in 4th grade. Fortunately, I had pretty good teeth. Did I have to be shipped off to camp for 8 weeks every summer? "Daddy and I will only be two time zones away." When my high school boyfriend pulled up in his Triumph Spitfire convertible, my mother's only outward show of concern was her rather peculiar comment, "Don't become a statistic!" as we tore down the street. Were there even seatbelts in that car? The expectation was that I would take care of myself. My parents would be there if needed, but they had confidence in my judgment, and so I began to have confidence in myself, too.

At the time, my life seemed to center far too much around my parents and their needs, and not enough on mine. After-school activities that involved my mother driving me anywhere were strongly discouraged, unless they coincided with her bridge schedule. Apparently, that's called "parent-centered child-rearing," and now I couldn't agree with it more. I'm actually evolving toward it, like a plant orienting itself toward the sun to survive. Perhaps my parents' approach had its merits after all. Not only do I understand their choices, I am actually starting to employ their methods.

I have thus far resisted the impulse to purchase a car that seats an inconveniently large number of occupants. In this way, I am happily unavailable for carpools or play dates, a phrase that makes my mother's eyes roll. Toothpaste no longer automatically appears on my kids' toothbrushes at bedtime. They fasten seatbelts and shut car doors all by themselves. When pressed, they can tie their own shoes. Any day now, I will begin to leave the milk and cereal on the table so that they can help themselves. I have given serious thought to rearranging the dishes in our kitchen so that their little fingers can reach their own glass of water/juice/beer, whatever. And, while I routinely witness friends cajoling their uncooperative son or daughter to eat a banana, patiently explaining the benefits of potassium, I have more or less stopped chasing my son around the kitchen with a forkful of brisket.

My children have their assigned chores, which, if not performed with alacrity, are at least not performed by me. Here is the (mostly truthful) list: making their beds in the morning (except when they are late to school), feeding the fish (except when they forget), setting the table (after a somewhat protracted battle) and unloading the dishwasher on the weekends (minus the really sharp knives). It sounds suspiciously like my own childhood.

On a recent visit, my mother observed my husband and me getting our kids ready for school. Perhaps she didn't entirely approve of the spoon-feeding breakfast technique or the play dead/mamma bear routine. In any case, she didn't intervene. It was a harmonious visit.

As I tick off another year on this planet, I must also reflect on what wisdom I may possibly have acquired in that time. Will I instill in my kids the same self-reliance that my parents did in me, simply by virtue of allowing me to make choices for my-self? I hope so, although I do intend to accompany them to the dentist for the foreseeable future, at least until the cavity-prone years are over. But in guiding my bright-eyed son and daughter into their own promising life adventures, I expect them to do their part as well. I can only hope to show resolve and good humor, with a dash of humility, in getting through this chal-lenging, wondrous thing called parenthood.

Chapter 4:

Standing Strong

Skimming the Surface
by Diane Compton

As I was flopping down a dock in flippers too big, I had no idea I was about to live a life-defining moment. Not a dramatic, make-or-break moment—there would be plenty of those to come. No, this moment, my first snorkeling trip, was more of a whisper, a small road sign easily missed. Honestly, my giraffe-like sprawl into the water and frantic silt-stirring treading as I defogged and vacuum-sealed my snorkeling mask felt more like embarrassment than enlightenment. In between gulps of salty water, I wondered what I had gotten myself into and why my new husband suggested this as fun. However, with my first glimpse underwater, my wondering instantly became wonderment. My awkward flippers suddenly became powerful and just the right size for exploring my new underwater world. A world I had unknowingly already been a part of, but could not see with my surface-skimming gaze. A world I had blindly stirred up and changed with my struggles to remain vertical.

From that moment on, I was hooked like a fishing enthusiast after the 6-foot barracuda we saw relaxing in shallow waters. Snorkeling was not the most convenient hobby for land-locked

Midwesterners, so my husband and I spent our first years of marriage traveling to snorkel.

We visited Hawaii, where the ocean taught me that if I relaxed into the big waves, they would support and guide me in a new direction before leaving with a gentle crest. If, however, I became tense, trying to return to the false-security of vertical, the ocean fought me, often tossing me into rocks and stinging creatures of various sorts.

In the Bahamas, I learned that even if required by law and enforced by officials in patrol boats, it is extremely difficult to snorkel with a life jacket. While the life jacket arguably saved me from drowning—I did survive the trip after all—it forced me to remain vertical. The ocean tossed me about like a cork, as I struggled to keep my head underwater to catch glimpses of the deeper and beautiful world that seemed to elude me.

Our last trip before children was to Australia, where we explored the Great Barrier Reef. All the other reefs we had visited were contained, the end of the reef easily in sight. Here, we were humbled as we became part of an underwater world that seemingly went on forever. We would need months, not hours, to explore fish, corals, and plants that only existed in this far corner of our world.

However, as our sense of adventure and wonderment became fulfilled through starting a family, our trips to the sea were taken via memories not airplanes. I did use snorkeling as my focal point, my happy place, when our first child was born. I relaxed into the waves, waiting for the gentle crest for 19 hours—it was a very big ocean. Our second child arrived via C-section, the life jacket of birth.

With children onboard, there was not a lot of time or money for snorkeling. The ocean's call was overshadowed by sleepless nights and joyful giggles. It was a good life, filled with the comforts of success and glorious typicalness. I had a good career, a great marriage, two amazing children—even strangers would comment on how well-behaved our children were and would call us the perfect family. Of course, I knew we were far from perfect—they hadn't watch us get ready for school after all—yet their comments gave me pride, like a manager taking credit for a team performance review. For the first time in my life, I was in control—or so I thought.

Our third child was an unexpected blessing we were told we couldn't have. Even before we had fully accepted the idea of three, we had our first of many "but wait, there's more," doctor appointments. We went from serious complications to worse. We were strongly encouraged to do the fair thing by aborting our daughter or refusing medical treatment so that she could die peacefully before birth. Genetic counselors, social workers, doctors, and nurses used that word, fair, over and over again—was it fair to our other children to bring a baby with needs into the home—was it fair to our marriage, our budget—was it fair to society to bring a child who will require special services and funds her whole life?

We prayed. We cried. We questioned. In the end, we knew this was our child, our children's sister, and she needed us. Just as we, or any parent for that matter, would provide medical treatment for our other children if they were hurt or sick—so would we help our littlest daughter. She wasn't any less our little girl just because we hadn't met her face-to-face yet.

With that decision, we began our journey to the Great Barrier Reef of parenting. Our fears seemed endless, yet so did the comforting kindness of people doing everything they could to help us. Nationwide prayer chains were formed. Baby gifts, notes of encouragement, and anonymous donations appeared daily.

As doctors predicted, Erin Faith arrived two months premature, with Down Syndrome and just about every complication that came with it. She weighed in at 3 lbs and required a major abdominal surgery on the first day of her life. A second abdominal surgery and open-heart surgery followed. Four months of her first year was spent in hospitals. Nights and days were filled with round-the-clock medications, feeding tubes, and oxygen monitors, as my husband and I obtained do-it-yourself medical degrees.

As we had predicted, Erin is a beautiful little girl, who, despite all she went through, smiled on January 22, 2005, two days after her original due date and on time according to the development charts. Now, at age three, Erin knows about 200 words in sign language, happily teaching them to others. She takes swimming and music classes, and is working on pre-reading skills. While we are still a long way from perfect, Erin has completed our family in a way no other child could.

With fewer medical concerns, we've had time to vacuum-seal our facemasks and see the amazing world around us—a world we had always been a part of, but didn't know. We had been skimming the surface, missing so much human goodness. Our two older children have the luxury of growing up in this world, easily accepting and loving their little sister. Their whole lives will be spent below the surface, growing up in the beauty of service and unconditional love. This year they both decided to use their birthday parties to raise money for kids with special needs. What started out as a small birthday party has grown into so much more, with people offering to help, making donations, and writing newspaper articles.

While I had originally feared strangers' comments and stares, I now know Erin would want it no other way. As she smiles, waves, and gives people her best "hiilo," I have the pleasure of watching their first glimpses into the underwater world we call home now. Most won't stay long, but others are changed forever by our little ambassador.

I also discovered a whole industry of people who chose to jump into the deep water to help those of us who are thrown in unexpectedly. From therapists to camp volunteers, our family is so grateful for people who somehow knew this deeper world existed and became its lifeguards.

I still do have moments where I try to return to the false-security of vertical, and I even sometimes mourn the loss of our easier, surface-skimming days. However, after crashing into a few rocks and stinging creatures, I relax into the waves, joyfully anticipating my new direction and waiting for the gentle crest.

Keys

by Tamara Madison

In the photo my children
    run along a wet shoreline
    on a bright day of whipping winds.
    Jagged cliffs of red stone and grey
rise like bleachers
above the flinging sand.

He is the young man in baggy shorts
and sunglasses, hair flying,
grinning wide as he runs,
leggy sister on his back.
Her hood tied round her face
is like a mouth pronouncing "cow,"
but you can see in the narrow patch
of light that shows only a peek of nose,
the inner corners of eyes, a touch
of upper lip, that she is grinning too.
Her legs dangling through his pocketed arms
are bare, strong-calved in blue gym shoes.

He has not yet climbed
the rocky island that rises unseen
behind them in the greenwhite frothing
surf, and I do not yet know
that my keys lie somewhere hidden
beneath the blowing sand,
that it will take an hour of worry,
the help of strangers, and finally,
an unbeliever's desperate plea
to Saint Anthony before the wind
will part the sand to reveal them,
the keys to everything else
that seems important in my life.

Flipping the Bird at Fear
by Amy Logan

To the ancients, the presence of a bird sometimes heralded the ascent of the soul to the gods, often via death. I wasn't thinking of such ominous foreshadowing the afternoon my son, Vaughan, first took notice of birds. We were walking with friends in a park that had recently been built between a new five-star resort and the ocean. I carried my fifteen-month-old son as we strolled amidst the sun-drenched gardens, sweet sage in the sea air. He pointed to a bird in the flowerbed and, as I stepped forward to give him a closer view, I felt a gush of air and saw a blur before my eyes. An electric service cart had just flown past us, mere inches from our faces. Two hotel maids had used the park sidewalk to get to the other end of the resort. They'd swerved to miss us, but didn't even look back, or stop to make sure we were okay.

It was a very close call. I'd been carrying Vaughan on one side, his head blocking my view from the direction the maids had come. His head would have been the first thing struck. My first instinct was to blame myself: Shouldn't I have been paying attention? But I didn't even know vehicles were allowed on these sidewalks. There were no signs to warn anyone. Electric carts are notoriously quiet, so I didn't hear it coming. I carried a growing pit in my stomach as we made our way home.

That evening, I replayed the incident over and over in my mind. At the speed the cart was going, Vaughan certainly would have died if we'd been hit. I would have been hospitalized. My father, a safety expert, said a pedestrian shouldn't have to walk that defensively on a park sidewalk. I thought of our recent family vacation at a Caribbean resort where its electric cart drivers waited for guests to wave them to pass safely.

My guilt turned to rage. I phoned the local resort and calmly relayed the incident to the manager. He promised to get back to me when he'd investigated it, but didn't apologize. When I mentioned the Caribbean resort's policy, his only response was to ask me how I liked that hotel—his brother-in-law was the manager of it.

I wrote to the local resort's CEO, who had his manager write me that the company regretted I was "frightened by the passing cart." There was still no acknowledgment or apology that their employee had actually done something dangerous. Our close call and its bitter aftermath haunted me. For three months, I suffered insomnia, nightmares, rashes and anxiety. I wondered if I would ever be okay again.

I'd had close calls before Vaughan was born, but none had ever left me so shaken. In a remote jungle of Costa Rica, I came within inches and seconds of stepping on a lethally poisonous snake, which I avoided only by a fluke. When I was climbing

Ayers Rock in Australia, someone higher up dropped a water bottle that whizzed by, inches from my head, as it plunged off the rock. Those events left me feeling lucky, not bereft.

Why it was different when it was my child, not myself, in harm's way, I'm still not sure, but I do know how such an experience served me: It all but killed my breast-feeding-induced oxytocin buzz, which awakened me from my fantasy that motherhood is all love and light. I realized that something tragic could actually happen to me—to my precious angel. There are real dangers out there, sometimes where we least expect them. Part of what it means to be a mother is the struggle to protect my child—because the world isn't always supportive of my plan. Along with his father, I am Vaughan's only true protector. And he needs me to be stronger than I ever thought I could be.

Most of all, I know now that, like birds, which my son has grown to adore, the safety of motherhood is fragile, fleeting, vulnerable and, yes, beautiful. Without the risk, there would be less reward. Anybody could raise a child well. Because life is risky, nurturing life is riskier. But you get to be exquisitely alive.

Encounters with birds are still sparking insights for me. Recently, I took Vaughan, now six, to the Wild Animal Park to feed the lorikeets. After a crowd left, the birds were full and cranky, but I found one up in a branch that was willing to drink the nectar I offered from a cup. When I extended a finger for him to perch upon, he bent down and bit me. "Ouch!" I cried, recoiling and spilling the nectar. Vaughan checked my finger. "He didn't break the skin, Mommy," he said. "It'll be okay." Then, he hugged me the way I do when he is hurt. And, indeed, that was enough for me to be more than okay again.

Boating, Skating
by Thelma Adams

On a balmy summer Sunday, we motored down the Hudson River in Jonathan's 25-foot sloop. The boat had one of those midlife names: the freedom, the liberty, the father of two feeling his mortality. We were four: Jon, his six-year-old Mark, my daughter Olivia and me. This was Livvy's first boat trip. Clutching her Barbie life-jacket, my six-year-old was fearless--not necessarily a good thing on a river. But water safety was the least of my worries.

Olivia has rosebud lips and curly spun-gold Rapunzel hair. She is an experimental dresser --very Britney Hilary Lindsay. That morning, Livvy wore a skimpy red T-shirt she'd outgrown in pre-school and red hip-huggers. Neither thick nor thin, she had the muscular body a child gets from running and swimming and Kung-fu fighting.

After Livvy and Mark took turns blasting the air horn and trailing an oar out the side of the boat, they clambered down below to the captain's bunk, a cushiony triangle at the boat's bow. Mark's father, an occupational therapist, steered us South toward the Esopus lighthouse. A wide-eyed Raggedy Andy with yellow ringlets, earnest Jon is studiously kind. His lack of any edge makes him appear clueless, although I didn't know him well enough to make this judgment.

While he discussed his recent passion for boating and the wonders of teak, I surveyed the mini-mansions on the Hudson's leafy Eastern bank. We talked in the way play-date-parents talk – unfamiliar adults accommodating their social children. Jon scouted locally for Brown University, and had inside dirt on various local high schools. We compared the relative merits of bigger schools versus smaller, prep versus public.

We were getting way ahead of our first-graders. It was suddenly strangely quiet down below. "I'll check on the kids," I said, descending the stairs. The accordion door to the cabin was shut. As I noisily un-snapped the door, the kids assembled themselves. Livvy reclined on the cushions; Mark kneeled beside her.

I asked my Livvy what they had been doing. Without confessing, they begged me to shut the accordion door.

"We've got a situation," I called through the hatch, "the kids are playing doctor." Jon smiled back nervously from his position on high by the rudder. I couldn't get parental traction with the guy.

"Do they want juice boxes?" Jon asked. If I had been more acute, I might have suspected he was enjoying my discomfort.

I strained to keep them on deck – and Jon did nothing to help. His passivity irked me. True to my generation, I believe in letting parents discipline their own children. When pressed, Jon played professional therapist: "this was just kids exploring their mini- sexualities. It's a recognized developmental stage. I can call my colleagues to confirm, if you'd like."

By noon, after a lot of heavy silence broken by the kids crunching through a large box of peanut butter crackers, we navigated back up the Rondout Creek. I wanted to get back behind the wheel of my Subaru Forester Turbo. Once I'd put the Hudson between us and the boys, I looked at Olivia. She was a stubborn little girl in a funk, perfectly willing to lean her head against the car door and slip into a nap to escape interrogation.

I worried that if I had so little control now, what was I going to do with my little beauty when hormones did start to rise? But what really frosted me was my irrational sense of male swagger: could it be that Jon was quietly proud of his little man? Was Jon passive because he saw nothing wrong in Mark's behavior – or had he been toying with me?

Six months later, on a sleety Saturday, I drove Olivia back across the river to the Saugerties hockey arena for Mark's seventh birthday. In her embroidered pink coat, she resembled Doctor Zhivago's Lara. I looked like Mr. Green Jeans in flannel-lined overalls.

When we entered the ice rink's party room, Mark looked up from the floor where he was being trussed up into goalie leggings. Livvy dropped a "hi" to him. No rush to be together. I avoided all but cursory contact with Jon. There was a subtle acknowledgement that we'd all gotten to know each other more intimately on the boat, and then withdrawn. While the kids saw each other daily at school, there were no more play-dates.

I don't do ice, so I laced Livvy up and retreated to the bleachers. She shuffled to the middle of the rink where she followed her own bliss. When it suited her, she completed the conga line of skaters led by a more agile Mommy. Meanwhile, Mark, who had been playing ice hockey since he was a toddler, zipped back and forth, oblivious to the pull of girls. He bashed into the walls sending up jets of shaved ice, wielding his hockey stick with confidence.

An hour later, Livvy skated off the ice and announced, "I want to join a hockey league here, Mommy." On the way out, she waved the inflatable hockey stick she got in the goody bag, which held her interest more tightly than the birthday boy. "Goal!" she yelled at the backs of her departing friends. "Goal," she cried as we crossed the parking lot. But she wasn't thinking "Score." Not Livvy, just me.

When Love Isn't Delivered With the Baby
by Karina Schmidt

Was it because of the painful birth that I felt I could not love my child? I was in labor for nine hours, breathing through an oxygen mask and oblivious to the drama going on around me because I was so worn out from the pain. I had tried pushing in a tub of warm, aromatized water but having to hang on to the sides to prevent myself from drowning was too much additional muscle work. Although I hate needles, I had welcomed the epidural after six hours and pushed some more. Finally, at 10 p.m., 20 hours after my water had broken, we decided on a cesarean. They showed me my baby, and I turned my head to vomit. I was too tired to even hold it in my arms.

Despite the reassurances I'd had from friends and relatives, I hadn't expected childbirth to be an easy thing. What shocked me more was the fact that it took me over a year to develop the loving mother-baby bond. I thought unconditional love was supposed to be delivered automatically at the same time as the baby. It wasn't. In the weeks following the birth, the pain only continued in the form of breastfeeding. I could have sworn the baby had teeth that secretly appeared when it attached to the breast. And I was producing too much milk for the little fellow. I had to warm, massage, express and moisturize a couple of times a day, and a couple of times at night. Every time my son cried out of hunger, I cried too, but out of fear. It hurt and I hated it.

It was a relief when I gave up trying to breastfeed after four weeks. It was surprisingly easy to forget all the physical pain, but the mental scar was deep. Over the following months, I discovered how much I resented him. I seemed to blame him for my bodily pains, fatigue, insecurity over weaning, fear of doing something wrong, boredom of a stay-at-home lifestyle, and loss of the man-woman relationship, as I slipped down in my husband's priorities to third place after baby and work.

As I fought these negative emotions within myself, I was easily overwhelmed by the sound of my son's screaming. I suffered breakdowns where I sobbed uncontrollably. My husband worked such long hours and we didn't have any family members nearby, so I was practically a single parent during the week. The patient, loving mother that I wanted to become fell farther from my reach every day. I was desperate to change but didn't know how.

Of course I had known that bringing up a child was a big responsibility, but the immensity of it only dawned on me after I had started to experience it personally. I had not expected parenting to be such an enormous task. The fear that I was not a good mother added more pressure and it was all the more difficult that it's a rather hush-hush topic, even between friends. I was an emotional wreck. Almost a year went by before we took any action.

We finally admitted that time wasn't going to solve our problems, so we got a babysitter. I rebelled in these hours of freedom, deliberately choosing to sit in baby-unfriendly areas and taking pleasure in jaywalking. My husband and I forced ourselves to have an evening out—cinema! cocktails!—once a week. I joined a gym that had childcare so I could sweat off the stress and relax in the sauna. I also started seeing a therapist and it felt good to finally be able to talk about my feelings.

I like to believe that I'm getting better at mothering, but it's a constant uphill battle. Almost every day, I struggle to suppress the negative and ugly emotions that threaten my good intentions. Will these feelings ever go away? I can cope better when I see less of him, but does that make any sense? I doubt that I'm the only one going through such difficulties, but other women just sing the praises of motherhood. Especially, it seems, to those without children. Who are these mothers trying to kid? Or do they really mean it?

Now in his terrible twos, my son pushes my moods to extremes, with a fondness for performing in front of a large audience. I'd be lying if I said I don't feel embarrassed or insecure when strangers throw me disapproving looks. But I need to choose my fights carefully, because my inner strength is in such short supply. I wonder if it's enough to see me through his teens and beyond?

You Will Know
by Sarah Teres

You will know the difference between a hungry cry and a cry from pain.

You will know the difference between a run-of-the-mill illness and when to call 911.

You will find a fierce place in your soul reserved only for moments when you have to protect your kids.

You will discover a wealth of reserves you never knew you had.

You will be able to run a three-minute mile just to catch your child before he reaches the street, or falls out of a tree.

You will be able to stay up for four nights straight with a sick child.

You will find inside yourself a wealth of knowledge you never knew you had.

You will find your way and everything will be okay in the end.

Happiness outweighs anxiety, smiles overrule tears, and there is great power inside motherhood. Power enough to get us through the sleepless nights. Power enough to grant our children wings and watch them learn to fly.

Damaged but not Destroyed
by Laurel Meister

I've moved more times in the last five years than I care to count. Some called us crazy when my husband and I sold our home near Seattle and decided to move, with our two-year-old-daughter, to a fixer upper in California when I was eight months pregnant. A part of me agreed with them—but I can handle this, I thought, I can handle anything. I am Wonder Woman after all.

While deep into remodeling, we brought a baby home to a mattress on a floor sprinkled with plastic pipe shavings. We slept in the shadow of a miter saw while our daughter slept on a mattress in the closet. She started preschool knowing more about drywall than any other three year old. Surrounded by mess and disorganization, I kept it together as we slowly continued our home improvements.

Just one year later our home was severely damaged by a massive landslide. Fate had sent us out of town that day. We were overjoyed at having avoided the obvious psychological damage that could have occurred had the children witnessed the destruction of their world. We quickly learned that, along with other damage, the children's bedrooms and all of their belongings had been crushed. A few days later our family and friends were given only fifteen minutes to enter our condemned home and retrieve as much as possible. They took items to friend's houses, a storage unit, and my parent's house. Only our necessities stayed with us. Our lives were suddenly splintered, and we were scrambling for a place to stay. How would I explain all of this to my children and their little smiling faces? How would I keep smiling?

We moved to a friend's "backyard structure" for a few weeks. That is truly the best description for it. Luckily it was all popsicles and sleepovers to the kids. I spent my time wondering how I was going to keep a sense of stability and some semblance of routine in our family life. I started wondering if I could, in fact, handle anything.

With as few of our belongings as possible, we moved to a house donated by a "perfect" stranger. I presented the kids with the concept of how wonderful people can be and how thankful I was for their kindness. We were living in a different town trying tirelessly to stay connected to our own community. Our daily lives were certainly different, but I kept things as normal as possible. We stayed there for five months.

Just before Christmas we moved to a doublewide trailer off a busy road. I began to stress the concept of "making memories." Don't mind Niagara Falls in the living room on rainy days or the jiggle of the entire trailer when the washer is on spin cycle. We were lucky to have a washing machine and a roof over our heads.

The following summer was stifling. We were parked on a lifeless sea of black asphalt, so we brought out the art supplies and painted a garden across the trailer. It was 98 degrees inside, so we got in the shower with our clothes on and the kids sat in plastic moving crates full of water. I was striving to make the best of it. I was exhausted from trying to stay positive. Memories were made as nearly a year passed.

We finally moved home after fifteen months. Even though cracks, dirt, massive disorganization, and debt surrounded us, we had a renewed sense of gratitude, definition of home, and appreciation of others. We witnessed examples of the kind of people we will strive to be. We were touched by selfless acts, support, and financial aid from complete strangers, heroes really. These memories will be with us forever.

Our natural disaster was a multi-faceted beast. With no such thing as landslide insurance or federal aid and a looming uncertainty of how things were going to turn out, I had to dig deep. I couldn't change the past, couldn't predict the future, so I focused on the present. I had to deal with it and deal well; little people were watching me.

Like our home, we were damaged but not destroyed. Fortunately super powers are not reserved solely for well-accessorized women wearing beautiful bustiers. Power can be found within ourselves, strength can be drawn from those around us, and determination can come from those little smiling faces full of faith. I believe we all have powers of comic book proportion. I only hope to be someone's hero someday.

Maybe I already am.

Chapter 5:

Our Sweet Salvation

Making People
by Crystal McKee

"Ugh. I'm never having kids."

I used to say that a lot when my cousins were climbing on my head like a bunch of strung-out monkeys. They were so sticky. And smelly. And boogery.

As I gazed into the eyes of my newborn son when I was nineteen, I experienced an emotion that I had never felt before: unconditional love. It manifested in the wonder and complete trust in his tiny face and the fiercely protective instincts that gave me the resolve to leave his abusive father, Dylan, when he was a month old.

I bundled him up and prepared to leave the hospital, and it hit me. It was up to me to make this tiny creature into a kind, responsible, capable man. I couldn't make pancakes or casseroles or knit, but I was supposed to help him be who he would ultimately become. I sat heavily on the hospital bed, watched him sleep and pressed the call button to summon the nurse.

She came in and checked his car seat. "It looks good. You're all set," she said as she turned to leave.

"What do I do?" I asked.

"With what?"

"What if I screw him up? What if he grows up and becomes a panhandler with dandruff and, and, bad oral hygiene. What if he hates me?" I took a deep breath. "Oh, my God. What if he becomes a Democrat?"

She laughed. "Crystal, you just love him with all of your might and always put him first, no matter what. Always put him first."

When his father blindsided me with a custody suit a month before his first birthday, I sold what meager possessions I had and begged family members I had never even met to raise the money for an attorney.

My lawyer's name was Vern. That should have been my first clue.

The judge announced that he was giving sole custody to Devon's father because I was struggling to attend college and working nights as a bartender. I died. My body moved and my brain functioned, but I wasn't among the living. Devon's father was charming, manipulative and one of the most evil people I had ever encountered. I would be lucky to ever see my son again.

Over the next few years, I moved through life and existed. I hired a detective when I had the money and I always came up empty. Devon's father and his girlfriend never stayed in one place very long and they paid cash. There was no paper trail, no help.

When I would talk about him and the questions would come, I would always defend myself.

"I don't know what I did to lose custody," I would answer.

"You had to have done something," was a common response.

"Oh, well, there was that one time, while I was on the corner waiting for a john and I killed that guy with my rolled up newspaper," I would bitterly retort. "Then I used his Zippo to set a bus full of nun's on fire."

Eventually, I stopped talking about Devon. I tucked his memory away in the only part of my heart that still beat and when people would ask, I would quietly answer, "I don't have children."

My phone rang in the fall of 2003.

"Hello?"

"Crystal? It's Dylan. If you want Devon, you need to come to Austin and get him tomorrow. I don't have any money and I can't afford a kid."

I never slept that night as I prepared to make the twelve-hour trip to Austin to pick up an 11-year-old boy that I knew nothing about. I knew that he needed my help and that would have to be enough for now.

Unable to sleep, I went to the grocery store and bought things I thought a boy would like. I had fifteen frozen pizzas, a box of Pop-Tarts and four boxes of Cap'n Crunch. The cashier was incredulous.

"I don't know what to get," I mumbled as tears threatened to overwhelm me.

A few hours later, I drove in silence as the sun rose and I littered the seat of my car with Red Bull cans. I nervously practiced what I would say to Devon and fretted about whether or not I should hug him or let him come to me. I knew he had been taught to hate me, or what he had been told I was.

When I parked in front of the run down motel, my heart sank. What kind of place was this for a child?

I got out of my car and walked toward the lobby. As I neared the door, I steeled myself for my long awaited encounter with this young man I didn't know. The nurse's words came back to me: Always put him first. I was resolved that no matter how much he loathed the mom he had been led to believe I was, I would nurture him and do everything I could to undo the hurts and disappointments he had suffered in his life. I opened the door and saw him sitting on a chair. I stopped in my tracks and held my breath. I felt a rush of love and dread and hope. I waited and we looked at each other uncertainly.

And then something miraculous happened.

This boy, this child who had been discarded so callously by his father and treated as a meal ticket for so many years, looked at me with the same wonder and trust I had witnessed all those years ago. He shyly moved forward and enveloped me in his arms, exposing his vulnerability and his incredible tenderness. As I cradled him like the baby I had held so long ago, and as the years of self-loathing and doubt melted away, I realized that although I had set out to save him, my son had instead saved me.

Give a Kid More Than One Parent, And You're Asking For Trouble
by Patty Friedmann

Smith College was a hotbed of feminism—think Gloria Steinem and Betty Friedan—but when I wrote in to the alumnae magazine in 1976 to say I'd had a baby alone, I dared the editor to print my news. Even the most liberated women didn't go that far in those days; never mind about "a woman without a man is like a fish without a bicycle."

I must have sensed my guiding principle one day would be true if I was making a move that was so radical for the times. And now I've spent 32 years learning my instinct was right.

Give a kid more than one parent, and you're asking for trouble.

It was easy to make the case for having a child by myself—especially if I had to walk around being defensive and mouthy. I was simply proving that giving a kid only one parent was the right path. To bolster my expertise, I did my homework, and I had anthropology, religion, history, arcane literature, and Greek mythology on my side. (Hey, I went to Smith.) Let's face it: if I invoke Margaret Mead, the Bible, and John Irving, who's going to argue with me? If I fast-talk, single parenthood is practically mandated by history and nature.

I'll start off with the Bible. Since I have a Jewish name, I'll skip the New Testament, though if you take one look at the Pieta, you can see right away that Mary was a very good mother under trying circumstances—and there's no one else standing around asking her for a beer. The Old Testament is loaded with begats and he-knew-hers; I'm sure a lot of kids were reared without two parents in the tent. If Ishmael hadn't been reared by a single mother, Palestinians wouldn't be throwing rocks at Israelis today.

Margaret Mead found illegitimacy (not a pejorative in my book) and divorce everywhere, Eskimos on seventh marriages before the age of 30. Kunta Kinte in *Roots* had a daddy who was heavy on ceremony, but that daddy had his own hut. In the animal world, seahorse fathers carry the load. In herds, after rutting season the mothers go off alone. (Remember Dumbo with all those women?) Earthworms and leeches just simply dispense with gender altogether. Single parents are usually the most interesting characters on the screen—from *Murphy Brown* to Rachel on *Friends* to Teri Hatcher before she got boring on *Desperate Housewives*. Literature is rife with single mothers, Tess of the d'Urbervilles, Jenny Fields, mother of Garp, Hamlet's mother Gertrude, Jocasta, Marmee. Just about the only mother we don't know much about is Norman Bates's mother. He probably had a father.

With all this cultural knowledge, what about the

empirical stuff?

Yes, I can safely say that I can add one Patty Friedmann to the list of characters who distinguished herself as a single parent. And then she went on to become living proof that if you give a kid more than one parent, you're asking for trouble.

It all started ingenuously enough in 1975. I was working on my doctorate in Denver, I was gaga over a man named John, and I was feeling a need to steal John's baby right that second because I knew instinctively that he was going to get away. Sure enough, John was going to make what's now been a lifetime commitment to his then-'roommate'—the person my daughter Esme once referred to as her "wicked stepmother Steve." I stole one sperm from John. Just one. It was all I needed, and I scurried back to New Orleans, a dissertation short of the degree. I had the child I wanted.

It was decades before Maury Povich and DNA labs would make that speedy little sperm an issue. John was not a parent. I was not asking for trouble.

In New Orleans, I was treated like a pariah, but I took it as a badge of honor. A Jewish girl (age 28) from a very wealthy family did not do such a thing. Absolutely no one accepted me; everyone looked askance at me. But I was a visionary. And I had a beautiful honeymoon with my glorious Esme, who was pretty eugenically stellar: John was dreamy-looking, at least to me, and he had 800 verbal SATs. Esme herself needed little explaining. "John helped me make you," I said, showing her a photo. "He put the head on?" she said. The abandonment of pure, blissful unweddedness was insidious. If you want to wreck unwedded bliss, get married.

When Esme came of nursery school age, the pariah game wasn't so much fun anymore. People whispered about her at the school gate. So when the first jerk came along and asked me to marry him, I said yes. I kept my maiden name, and hyphenated Esme's. I wasn't hiding anything: I was just putting a daddy in the school directory. She told me years later that when he came to the door the day before our wedding she saw his arrival as punishment for something she had done wrong. His presence in her life has taken a terrible toll.

Marry in haste, repent at leisure. He was a bully. He was a milquetoast with an abusive streak, but in those days a marriage counselor would say, "You provoked him to hit you by crying." Esme and I stayed stuck on that glue-trap for 17 years, during which he and I adopted a baby boy after my body was lucky enough not to be able to hold onto babies he sired. The baby boy, Werner, was born with a sweet spirit. But Werner picked up a lot of his father's blustering ways. It almost took an exorcism to rid him of them. If only I had reared each of my children alone, I know they would be different. Happier.

I'm the single mother of two adult children now. Naturally they have rebelled against me and chosen to immerse themselves in loving marriages with children. After all I did for them, blazing a trail, helping to create a generation in which it is possible to rear children alone, free of stigma, free of an extra parent, basking in the pure romance of unwed parenthood.

This is what I get.

When I look at their in-laws, who are married couples, I see they have twice the resources to help out. But I also don't have a papa in my house who throws the kid up to the ceiling until her head hits. Or gives her sips of whiskey. And says he's taking her hunting when she turns six. My granddaughters see only me—me, Omie!—when they come to this side of the family. I've come full circle since 1976. I've got the big payoff. Those splendid little girls are mine, all mine!

He Changes Too
by Ingrid Miller

Motherhood changes dads. Just ask my husband, Chris.

As if the first year of parenthood was not hard enough, Casey was born prematurely, soon after McKayla. Months in the hospital were followed by weeks of around the clock medications at home. When the dust settled, I only had energy for the girls. There was nothing left for Chris who had morphed from my soul mate into a 6 foot 4 inch bundle of needs. At that point I wanted a husband who was like a chair; comfortable, good looking, useful—something I didn't have to fuss over.

Chris was not a very good chair. He kept insisting that I had changed. He wanted the "old" me back. Was he kidding? Parenthood had swallowed me whole and there was no going back. I wondered if he would be coming along for the ride.

As other parents hired babysitters and found time for themselves, we remained at home. The girls reacted poorly to crowds, noise and strangers so babysitters were out. Chris had to adjust. He wondered if he was ever going to get me back.

Then McKayla was diagnosed with Autism and we nearly

drowned in grief. We had to educate ourselves. We scrambled to correct as many of the symptoms as possible, but evaluations, therapies and special education did not change her into a normal child.

As we mourned for the dreams that would never come true, McKayla made progress on her own schedule. She was quite content with her "special" brain. It took time for us to accept her limitations and in so doing; we became more accepting of each other.

Chris hung in there, loved us and paid the bills. Thank goodness he was not a chair. We needed him to be so much more than that. He was the foundation of our lives. He was actually a large, stable rock.

Joined
by Donna Hilbert

Our kitchen, winter Sunday
boys playing on the floor,
I'm drying breakfast dishes
when I have the vision:
four chairs in front of a store
on a street I never travel.
Four chairs that will complete
our chair-less dining room suite.
I drive into the vision
and they are there,
with the same turned legs,
the same dark wood
as our furniture at home.
And on the bottom of one seat:
1927, date in the same hand
as on the table, underneath.

Everything sundered
wants reuniting,
everything rent, to mend.

So, I am not amazed Dear Heart
that nightly you walk
from the occluded country
to rest awhile with me.
Are not we
who have born three sons,
more joined than chair and table
turned from a single tree?

Am I Blurry?
by Sheila Golden

One unusually cold evening in Southern California, I was standing in our driveway watching Owen, my six-year-old son, whiz by on his bicycle. He had recently mastered the two-wheeler, although a little late getting the hang of it. Blame it on the divorce, the alternate weekends, and the different styles in "coaching."

His father prefers the push you hard from behind and let you fly down the street hoping you take flight or freight and remain upright technique. Owen most often ended up parallel to the ground, spirit broken and slightly banged up. My approach was to hang on to the fender for dear life and run behind with my forty something, out of shape thighs, rotating as fast as possible all the while smiling, just in case the neighbors happened to be watching.

Interesting differences, the father pushing his son to move ahead with confidence and speed and the mother clinging to the back fender making sure there is a painless and successful transition.

The early toddler years are especially hard, some things get better with parenthood and others take on a new life form. All of a sudden your living room is filled with play date moms, a subculture I hadn't known existed. These women whom you have absolutely nothing in common with, other than children relatively the same age, are now who you spend the larger part of your waking hours with.

The same women that you would likely never choose to have over for coffee pre-baby are now sitting on your couch and you are hosting them and their children for hours on end. As their toddlers tear your house apart you watch in disbelief and flash a pinched smile with eyebrows raised as far as they will go, and simply say, "It's okay."

As you shut the door behind these people you slump down in your chair and cry a good hard cry. You're not quite sure what the tears are about, just that somewhere along the way, you've lost yourself. This wasn't at all how you imagined it would be. No one is really interested in who you are anymore, or what you did prior to being "here." You are all equals in the play-date world.

You tell others about your exciting career life, the one where you wore great shoes and traveled the world. "I was a fashion editor. I worked in the commercial industry." No one cares. Is Owen potty trained yet? Does he sleep through the night? Can he count to 100? Recite the constitution? Speak a foreign language?

What I do know for sure is that motherhood has taught me to be kinder to myself, to forgive myself, and to be compassionate with myself. I used to never leave the house without mascara or my hair done. I worked out and wore high heels. When I meet someone in the grocery store that I haven't seen in years her eyes widen in disbelief. "Yes it's really me!" I want to scream, "I haven't slept through the night in years—I'm busy doing nothing and everything."

Then one day you notice you got through the week without complaining or shedding a tear. You start sleeping a few more hours, replacing those long and sleepless nights where you fantasize about sleeping, instead of having actual fantasies. You wear underwear that is pretty again, instead of secretly putting on those big cotton panties you bought during pregnancy, hoping not to be in a car crash and prove your mother right.

As I stood watching Owen racing by, his little legs going as fast as humanly possible, he shouted, "Am I blurry?"

He turned around a few houses down and raced past me again "Am I blurry?"

My eyes welled up. I felt so perfect in that moment as I realized that having a child fills in those tiny cracks in your heart.

And yes, he was blurry.

Letter to the Mother of That Baby
by Judy Berna

Dear Young Mother,

I am walking down the mall right now, thinking of you, and the encounter we had just minutes ago. I noticed you stiffen up as I approached your baby and how uncomfortable you seemed when I asked you how old he was and where he got that gorgeous blond hair. I know full well how 'times have changed' and every stranger is a threat of some unknown virus or a potential baby abductor. But I wanted you to know who I am, and why it meant so much to me to spend just a minute with your precious child this afternoon.

I am a grandmother who has a handful of wonderful grandbabies who I am lucky to see once or twice a year. They live a thousand miles away, but it may as well be a million. I miss them so much and regular phone calls and photos in the mail can only do so much to quench my longing for them. By admiring your baby I can almost imagine that he is my own grandson, and I can picture in my mind how he would smile if I had the chance to coo at him.

I am a thirty-year-old woman who has tried for eight years

to conceive a baby of my own. I have the most adoring, loving husband, who would make the perfect father, if only my body would cooperate. It is hard for me to see your baby and know how blessed you are. Yet it is comforting for me to see him, to know that the God who gave him to you is the same God I trust. His precious smile will come to mind later this week when I have yet another unwanted period.

I am a newlywed who is so excited to be married to the man of my dreams, but almost ready to move on to the next phase in our life together. I wonder how your life is, what it is really like to be that baby's mommy. I chatter at your son and play the video in my mind of what it would be like to be responsible for him. I wonder so many things, and know you have just experienced a lot of them in the last year. What will it be like to feel a person kicking you from the inside? How much does labor really hurt? Is it really possible to maintain a friendship in our marriage once we become our parents? The time I spent with your son today will leave me pondering these questions for the rest of the afternoon.

I am a mother too. My baby died of SIDS a year ago. It was over six months after we lost him before I could allow myself to even go to the mall. Every baby there was a reminder of the one I was not lugging around. I hated the idea of not needing to make sure the stroller was in the car before we left for errands. At first I would not allow myself to look into anyone's stroller. When I finally did I was surprised at how healing it was to see the cherub cheeks and twinkling eyes. I was reminded that it was because my son was so precious that I miss him so deeply. I was reminded that God is still in the business of making babies and maybe one day he would bless us again, and give us a sibling for our first angel baby. I needed your son's smile to lift my spirits today; thank you for sharing him with me.

I am the mother of three children myself but my youngest is now in the second grade and it seems like fifty years ago that she was the toddler, just learning about the wonders of the mall. I wonder how, so quickly, I can go from being the one on that side of the stroller, to the one on this side. I gaze into your son's face and see every one of my baby's innocent features. I feel a deep sadness that my days of being a baby's mommy are gone forever and in the two minutes that our paths crossed today I got to re-live for a moment the wonderful joy that a baby's smile can bring.

I am the mother of three beautiful girls and your son intrigues me. We are finished with having babies and I can honestly say we are blessed to have such wonderful, healthy children. But I have to also admit that I do wonder, on days like today, when I see a precious little baby boy, what it would be like to mother one of the male variety. I wonder if his temperament is more laid back, if he cries less, if he lives up to all the stereotypes that are placed so flippantly on male children. I don't dare ask, for fear that someone would accuse me of not 'wanting' my third daughter, but I do wonder. I mean no harm to your son; he just fills me with questions.

I am the mother of two preschoolers. You would think I

would be the last person who would want to take time to speak to your baby, since I have several at home myself. But I am drawn to his chubby cheeks for a different reason. We have discussed so many times whether or not to have just one more. We are so happy with our first two and hate to upset the balance, but the things my body says to me when your son smiles makes me wonder if I am as done as I used to think. I wonder silently how having him in our household would change things, for the better or worse. I will walk away pondering silent questions your son raises in my mind.

So you see, there just may be that occasional bad guy out there, but it is not me. I have my own reasons for wanting to spend a minute with your child, and none of them involve dashing to the nearest exit with him under my arm. I understand your fears, and will respect them any way I can. All I ask is that you realize who I am too, and where I am coming from. And know that your son's smile could just make my whole day.

With a smile still on my lips,
One Shopped Out Lady

What Love Does
by Patti Callahan Henry

Motherhood births humility and destroys arrogance. This I believe. Although it is a rude awakening, it isn't the one thing I wish someone had told me about being a mother; I'll get to that soon. But this was the first lesson I learned after giving birth to a blue-eyed daughter, Meagan, fifteen years ago. Now, before we get too far into this story, let me offer some background. I'm a pediatric nurse with a master's degree in Child Health. I knew this Mom-Thing would not be as big an adjustment for me as it obviously was for others. I mean, please, I went to graduate school for this.

Well there you go, humility as a by-product of the destruction of arrogance. By the time Meagan was ten days old, I had hit the cold stonewall of my own limitations. Ten days were just long enough to crush eight years of advanced education, and nine months of confidence in my mothering skills. I really had no idea what I was doing or how I would care for another living, breathing human being. No one told me how tired I would be; how four hours sleep would sound like a full night; how taking a shower would be the only thing I would check off my to-do list on some days. I was lost, exhausted and wondering what I had done to my life.

Then my mother-in-law came to visit. This sounds like the setup for a bad joke, but not this time. She came into our home and insisted that my husband, Pat and I take a few hours alone—go to dinner and movie. This sounded like paradise, so I took her up on it.

I entered the movie theater with the selfish motive of eating buttered popcorn, enjoying two quiet hours and having an adult hand to hold. In my fog of fatigue, I made a meager attempt to watch the movie, to understand the plot and dialogue. Yet, what I ended up doing was this: wondering if Meagan needed to nurse; worrying if my mother-in-law had used the right diaper cream; believing a fire would break out and engulf the house while I was gone; being convinced that an escaped prison convict would run to my home for refuge. Yeah, this was fun.

Worries I'd never encountered ran through my mind like strangers entering without permission. Then the emotion hit me in the solar plexus: I would never again, for the rest of my living life, worry about only myself again. Ever. This, I thought, this is what love does: makes self less and someone else more.

This thought brought such wonderment and engulfing change that I was overcome with pure love. Nothing would be the same from this moment forward. Every move I made, every decision I pondered, every thought that moved through my mind would now pass through the love I had for my child (and later, children).

An awareness of a life more important than my own, a life I valued above all other life, has hit me at various times since then, but that night in the movie theater with a ten-day old daughter at home with her grandma, was the first time.

And this is what I wish someone had told me about being a mother. Listen, Patti, you think you know love now? You think you love with everything you have? Just wait. This love, this love for your child, allows you to do things you thought you could never do, makes you want to be a better person than you think you can be. This love is a reflection of a greater love than your own.

That, right there, is what I wish someone had told me.

Before we were mothers, how could we have known that the only way we would be able to sacrifice spirit, sleep, time, career, and self would be with a love so great we couldn't explain it to another?

Some years later, I went on a ski trip with a group of our friends. I sat at a table with people I'd known for years. A woman leaned across the table and asked how motherhood was treating me. Fine, I answered, and then I told her that no one had ever told me I would love this much. She, being a mom, answered in agreement with tears in her eyes. Another woman, one without children yet, asked me how I had given up my career after so many years of school.

My heart swelled with agape, and I replied. "This is what love does."

Indeed, this is what love does.

About the Contributors

Thelma Adams has been *Us Weekly's* film critic since 2000, after six years reviewing at the *New York Post.* She has twice chaired the prestigious New York Film Critics Circle. She has written for *The New York Times, O, Marie Claire, More,* I*nterview Magazine,* and *Self.* She has appeared on CNN, E!, NY1, NBC's *The Today Show,* CBS's *The Early Show,* Fox News Channel, *Access Hollywood, Entertainment Tonight,* Bravo and VH1. In 1993, she earned an MFA in fiction from Columbia University; she graduated Phi Beta Kappa from UC Berkeley in 1981. She lives in Hyde Park, New York, with her husband, son, daughter, four cats, one spaniel and a herd of wild turkeys.

Mary Helen Berg, mother of three children, lives in Los Angeles with her husband and their labradoodle, Boomer. Berg is a freelance writer whose essays have appeared in the *Los Angeles Times* and *Newsweek.* Currently at work on several books for children, Berg says if she could learn to write while she drives, she would be very prolific indeed.

Judy Berna is a mom who has it all: four children with a nice variety of personalities, one archaeologist husband who still loves her old bones, one extra large poodle, one stuck-up cat who licks inappropriate places only when company is over, one job working with Alzheimer's patients who keep her in touch with her forgetful side, and one amazing artificial leg that works so well it lets her keep up with the whole gang. She and her accomplices have lived in several glorious states of our union including Missouri, New Hampshire, Washington D.C., Utah, and most recently upstate New York.

Diane Compton lives in Illinois with three amazing children and her husband. She left a marketing job in the corporate world to start a more family-friendly computer training business. Diane has dual degrees in English and Computer Science from North Central College and a Masters in Communications from Northwestern University. At the moment, she is pursuing an advanced independent study degree in family management, taught by three of the best instructors in the world. Diane is currently helping to start a Gigi's Playhouse Literacy Satellite site in her town. This program provides free tutoring and personalized curriculum to children with Down Syndrome and their families. Learn more at *gigisplayhouse.com.*

Jennifer A. Davis was raised in Southern California. After graduating from high school, she attended the University of San Diego, where she received her BA in English along with her Teaching Credential. After teaching English at the high school level, Jennifer quit to become a full-time mother. She now has three beautiful children, four years of age and younger. When Jennifer isn't taking care of her kids, she enjoys writing. Her lifelong dream is to have a book published. She is currently working on her first novel (which is coming along very slowly with three young kids). Jennifer and her family currently reside in Escondido, California.

Pat Dunnigan is a Chicago-area freelance journalist, writer and editor whose work has appeared in *The Tampa Tribune*, *The Boston Globe*, *Florida Trend*, *American Lawyer*, *The Miami Daily Business Review* and the *Almanac of Florida Politics*, among other places. In 2007, after more than a decade of writing about trends in law, politics and business, she began taking herself a lot less seriously, launching the website Suburban Kamikaze, where her essays on parenting, sex and laundry have attracted a small, cult-like following. She lives in the Chicago suburbs with her husband and their two children.

Barbara Eknoian's first collection of poetry, *Jerkumstances*, won the Jane Buel Bradley Chapbook Award and was published by Pearl Editions in 2002. A veteran of Donna Hilbert's poetry workshop in Long Beach, she was nominated by Michael Hathaway, editor of *Chiron Review*, for a Pushcart Prize in 1996 and 1997. She resides in a lively household, with husband, children and grandchildren in La Mirada, California.

Patty Friedmann is the author of six darkly comic literary novels set in New Orleans: *The Exact Image of Mother, Eleanor Rushing, Odds, Secondhand Smoke, Side Effects*, and *A Little Bit Ruined*, as well as the humor book *Too Smart to Be Rich*. Her titles have been chosen as Discover Great New Writers, Original Voices, and Book Sense 76 selections. She has published reviews, essays, and short stories in *Publishers Weekly, Newsweek, Oxford American, Speakeasy, Horn Gallery, Short Story, LA LIT, Brightleaf, New Orleans Review*, and *The Times-Picayune* and in anthologies *The Great New American Writers Cookbook, Above Ground, Christmas Stories from Louisiana, My New Orleans, New Orleans Noir*, and *Life in the Wake*. Her stage pieces have been part of *Native Tongues*. With slight interruptions for education and natural disasters, she always has lived in New Orleans.

Leesa Gehman is a single mom who lives vicariously through her friends. However, she does find the humor in the not-so-vicarious. She lives with her son (who's now six years old and is terribly embarrassed when his mom writes anything about him, especially involving poop or things he's stuck up his nose, even if it is funny), a spastic dog named Betsy and boring cat named Spaz. She has had nonfiction essays published in several parenting magazines and in the upcoming Seal Press anthology, *How to Fit a Car Seat on a Camel: And Other Misadventures Traveling with Kids*.

Anne Glamore is the author of the popular blog, *"Tales From My Tiny Kingdom."* She has also written for *iVillage,* Lipstick and Portico. She practices law in Alabama, where she lives with her husband and three sons, as well as a rotating menagerie of animals. She is lowbrow and highbrow, loving *The New Yorker* just as much as *Us Weekly.* She and her husband do not have a television in their bedroom, and she has never seen an episode of *Law & Order, CSI* or *Survivor.* She Jazzercises religiously. She is big on bargains but cautions that name-brand garbage bags are always worth the money. "Anne Glamore" is not her real name.

Sheila Golden recently purchased roller skates with pink wheels, loves name brands with deep discounts, gardening, and anything verbena. She never got the hang of smoking, sees life through a fisheye lens, is secretly afraid of clowns, read *The Fountainhead* and suddenly understood, always wanted to be The Flying Nun, considers herself a "bottom feeder" at estate sales, loves a good font, prefers cupcakes to cake, and feels there is a right way to fold towels and sheets.

Kate Hasenauer lives in Portland, Oregon, where she is a stay-at-home mother to three children. Her husband has been searching for the right job in the right city somewhere in the USA and has taken the family along for the ride. Kate's goal is to provide a loving, healthy, structured and fun environment for her family and to someday write a short story collection. Some days she feels like a success. Other days she is horrified when she thinks about the amount of chocolate she's given her children. Prior to starting a family, Kate lived in New York City and worked in book publishing and then outside of Detroit, Michigan, where she worked as a copywriter.

Patti Callahan Henry is the national bestselling author of five novels with Penguin/NAL, including *Losing the Moon, Where the River Runs, When Light Breaks,* and *Between the Tides. The Art of Keeping Secrets* will be released in June of 2008. Patti has been short-listed for the Townsend Prize for Fiction and has been nominated for the Southeastern Independent Booksellers Fiction Novel of the Year. As a minister's daughter, she learned early how storytelling affects our lives. Before having children, she worked as a Clinical Nurse Specialist. She is a full-time writer, wife and mother, living with her husband and three children outside Atlanta on the Chattahoochee River, where she is working on her sixth novel. Learn more at *patticallahanhenry.com.*

Donna Hilbert's new poetry collection, *The Green Season,* will be published by World Parade Books in late 2008. Earlier books include T*raveler in Paradise: New and Selected Poems,* as well as *Transforming Matter, Deep Red* and *Women Who Make Money and the Men Who Love Them* (short stories), winner of England's Staple First Edition biennial prize. She and her poetry star in the short film, "Grief Becomes Me," the first in a trilogy to be included in the forthcoming documentary *Earthy Ties.* She lives in Long Beach, California, where she conducts a master class in poetry. Learn more at *donnahilbert.com.*

Geri Jacobs was born and raised in New York City. She attended City College, where she studied English Literature and Education. After her children were of school age, she received a Master's Degree in Art Education with encouragement and help from her husband. She was selected to participate in the Federal Magnet Program as a Drama, Music and Art specialist. Producing plays, conducting the school chorus, and publishing children's poetry were her passions. She currently volunteers as a docent for children at The Brooklyn Museum and The Metropolitan Museum of Art. Her two granddaughters are her inspiration for writing.

Cynthia Jenkins (also known as "Sugar Mama") is an award-winning parenting columnist and celebrity writer living in Laguna Beach, California. When asked what inspires her writing, she's quick to answer, "a good laugh." Living in a house with no backyard with a husband and two young sons, she prides herself on having plenty of material. But Cynthia is also known for tackling some of the tougher issues – parenting, friendship and life – with a sense of grace and diplomacy. (And if she's nailed it, a chuckle.) Learn more at *parentingoc.wordpress.com.*

Elaine Greensmith Jordan is a child of the Fifties. She had planned to teach and then stay at home, have babies and raise them to be exceptional people. Then life intervened. She divorced, got a degree in religion, adopted two children, and turned into an essayist. Her essay "Great Art and the Gods," was featured in the *UUWorld Magazine for Unitarians*. She won a prize from American PEN Women for a piece about her life as a mommy and published another mommy-piece in a *Cup of Comfort* anthology. Most of her work is about her eleven years as a Congregational minister, or about her life as a frustrated, ignorant, hysterical mom. It seems suffering has a readership.

Suzanne Jurva is a filmmaker, entrepreneur, wife and mom to two teenagers. She has been involved in all forms of storytelling, from Tom Hanks' IMAXfilm *Magnificent Desolation: Walking on the Moon* to producing for the smallest media - the mobile phone. In between the two extremes of media and technology, Suzanne was a feature film executive at DreamWorks, working on several Academy Award nominated films, including *Saving Private Ryan, Amistad, Minority Report, AI, The Lost World, Gladiator, Prince of Egypt, The Peacemaker, Deep Impact, Men in Black* and *The Lookout*. Her next goal is to get a large endorsement deal from a major shoe company and become a professional athlete.

Frank Leggett is an adventurer, world traveler, rock star, and home-dad of the past three years. He has two children, a very understanding and hard-working wife, a slowly deteriorating house, and a delusion that 47 is still not too old to have a hit single. He spends so much time driving kids to school, soccer practice, ballet class, shopping malls, swimming pools, play dates and birthday parties that he has a permanent seat-shaped curvature of the spine. He thinks he likes movies, parties, travel, live music, pubs and cocktails, but it has been so long since he experienced any of them, they are but a dim memory. One day, he hopes to read a newspaper and drink a cup of coffee without being interrupted.

Leigh Kaufman Leveen lives in Los Angeles with her husband and two kids. Prior to motherhood, she worked in the entertainment industry. In her early days as a development executive, she was involved with high profile features, including *Courage Under Fire*, *Eraser*, and *Daylight*. She has also written and produced several shows for the Biography series on A&E, two of which won a Cine Golden Eagle Award in 2005. Leveen is at work on her first novel; she hopes to finish it before the kids go to college.

Amy Logan has published articles and photographs in *The Los Angeles Times*, *The New York Times Sunday Magazine*, *The Dallas Morning News*, *The Denver Post*, *Parabola Magazine*, *Vegetarian Times* and other publications. Tribune

Media Services nationally syndicated her travel column, "Road Scholar." She is the author of the forthcoming novel *The Seven Perfumes of Sacrifice*, a thriller about the search for the divine feminine in the Middle East. She lives in California with her husband and son.

Tamara Madison grew up on a citrus farm in Mecca, California, and began writing poems as soon as she could hold a pen. Her work has appeared in numerous literary journals in the U.S. and United Kingdom. Her chapbook, *The Belly Remembers*, won the Jane Buel Bradley Chapbook Award in 2004 and was published by Pearl Editions. She lives with her daughter and their vicious pit bull in Los Alamitos, California. Tamara holds a Bachelor of Science degree in Linguistics from Georgetown University with a minor in Russian, and she teaches French at a no-longer-completely-failing high school in Los Angeles.

Crystal McKee is a wife to one very patient husband and mother to three children. She is also a frequent visitor to the land of Zoloft. She lives near Memphis, Tennessee, where she is a free-lance writer by night and an unruly cog in the gears of the GNP by day. Crystal began keeping diaries at the tender age of seven when she mistakenly thought that someone would someday care about the epic battle between her Barbie and Ken. She attended college in Austin, Texas, where she majored in business because she didn't know any better. Learn more at *BoobsInjuriesandDrPepper.com*.

Laurel Meister holds a bachelor of Fine Arts Degree in Illustration from Art Center College of Design. When not chasing her smiling children at the local park she is painting murals, illustrating children's books (e.g. *Tutu Knows Best*), selling her work at art fairs or online, and daydreaming about having time to publish her own illustrated children's story. Using her prestigious position as Mother to her advantage, she gathers inspiration from her two young children and infuses it into her whimsical artwork. Learn more at *whimsicle.net*.

Ingrid Miller joyfully gave up her law career when she became a mom. She grew up in Laguna Beach, where she was the first female ocean lifeguard. After her daughters were born, she returned to athletics to keep her sanity. She started with marathons and is currently training for her first Ironman Triathlon. She has written about autism on her website and for several running magazines. She resides with her family and menagerie of pets in Irvine, California. Learn more at *shutdownsandstressinautism.com*.

Regina Nervo's first book of poetry, *Oceanus*, was published by West-Coast Bias Press and released in the spring of 2008. Her poetry was also published in *City by The Sea*. She teaches school in Long Beach, California, where she lives with her husband and two children.

Mary Anne O'Connell was born in Chicago but now lives in southern California with her husband and two children. She is a registered nurse who started nursing school when she was pregnant with Baby No. 1. Ten years later (with the love and support of her family) she graduated! Today she works per diem at an outpatient surgery center primarily dealing with the geriatric population. During her days off, she works as a hospice volunteer, providing unconditional love and support to those in need at the most important time in their lives. Mary Anne enjoys traveling with her family to fun places like Costa Rica and Australia. She loves to cook, drink good wine, and eat chocolate.

Peggy Rambach is the author of the novel *Fighting Gravity*, and a collection of stories. She is the editor of two anthologies, *All That Matters: Memoir From the Wellness Community of Greater Boston* and *Seeds of Lotus: Cambodian and Vietnamese Voices in America*. Ms. Rambach has received numerous grants and fellowships for her writing and for her work as a teacher and artist in the healing arts. She lives in Andover, Massachusetts.

Angela Sandelier is a certified public accountant whose life and budget are not quite balanced. She was born in Missouri, grew up in Virginia, and went to college in Illinois. After living for a bit in North Carolina, she finally moved back home to Virginia where she lives with her gorgeous husband, two angelic children (ages 3 and 5) and the all-important family dog. Her career path started in public accounting, veered off into law firm management, non-profit accounting, for-profit accounting and back to where it all started, working those dreaded tax-season hours. When not slaving away on audits, you can find her updating her three blogs. Her other hobbies include reading, scrap booking, watching *The Biggest Loser* (what she wouldn't give to be trained by Bob and Jillian) and getting tattoos. She dreams of one day getting caught up on her sleep.

Karina Schmidt has spent her life collecting air miles, living in five countries and traveling to nearly forty. For the past two years, however, she has lived under house arrest in Germany. The computer has become a particularly close acquaintance and plays a pivotal role in achieving this year's goal: to become a writer. She's also busy learning how to become a good mother, whatever that might be. She's decided that she'll start by throwing amazing birthday parties.

Sarah Teres is the publisher of *Motherwords* Magazine, a new irreverent magazine dedicated to the reality and honest truth about motherhood. Previously, she was the editor-in-chief of *The Mother Connection*, a periodical for new mothers in the Merrimack Valley region of Massachusetts. Before becoming a mother, Sarah was an assistant at *Entertainment Weekly*, an actress in California, an English teacher in South Korea and a writer/editor for high school and college textbooks. Sarah is married and lives in Andover, Massachusetts with her three children, two cats, many fish and a tree frog. You can reach her at *sarah.teres@motherwords.org*.

Gloria Zimmerman lives in Los Angeles with her husband and their 7-year-old twins. Prior to becoming a stay-at-home mom, she traveled extensively, spoke at least two foreign languages and wore nice clothes to the office. In the distant past, she worked in the former Soviet Union, then in the film business as an assistant and eventually as an independent producer. She now teaches English as a second language, getting paid to foster independence in others. She is also learning to play mahjong, so far unsuccessfully.

About the Designer

Jan Schrieber is a professional graphic designer and wannabe photographer and illustrator who dreams of one day creating a children's book with her husband, a high school English teacher. A true nature lover and eco freak, Jan spends her 'me time' mountain biking and enjoying the Southern California waves. She has illusions of becoming a more confident surfer, so that when her children take to sea one day, she will be able to protect or embarrass them-whichever one comes first. This lovable surfer mama currently resides in Laguna Beach, California with her poetically hunky husband and two imaginative young grommets. See more of her work at: *www.graphicmuse.com*

About the Editor

Christine Fugate first dreamed of writing a column when she was a young girl and read Erma Bombeck and Ellen Goodman in the local Kentucky paper. She started writing Mothering Heights three years ago after submitting an essay about her plastic storage container habit to *The Laguna Beach Independent.* Since then she has written about almost every aspect of her life, including her addiction to chocolate, lack of style and obsession with her post-partum fat that lingers six years later. Two years ago, she started the popular website, *MotheringHeights.net,* to be in touch with other moms who enjoy writing about the parental state of mind.

For the past fifteen years, she has directed and produced award-wining films for VH1, Discovery Channel, Disney and her company, Café Sisters Productions. After she asked Julie Andrews the same question three times thanks to toddler–induced sleep deprivation, she decided to take a small hiatus from the Hollywood scene. She recently completed "The Peace Pole Project Song," a music video for the World Peace Prayer Society, a division of the United Nations, and is currently at work on *Earthly Ties*, a short film exploring poetry, motherhood and creativity.

She hopes to return to her passion for travel and tasting breads from around the world. Until then, she currently lives either in front of her laptop or in the kitchen where she cooks allergen-free meals for her husband and two daughters.

Christine can be found at
Mothering Heights.net or
ChristineFugate.com.

Acknowledgements

With gratitude as delicious and sweet as a chocolate ganache truffle, I would like to acknowledge the following people in my life who have helped me on my journey as a mother and writer.

My deepest thanks to all the women who answered the call for essays for the 2nd Annual Mother's Day Contest with their wise and funny words. Selecting the essays for the book was not an easy task. Without your words and hard work as mothers, we would not have this book and the online anthology.

Thank you to Stu Saffer and Andrea Adelson who gave me my first column in The Laguna Beach Independent and Mothering Heights its first readership.

Thank you to my readers, online and in print. Without you, I would have given up a long time ago.

Thank you to Erma Bombeck and Nora Ephron who taught me how to laugh with words.

Thank you to Susan McNeal Velasquez who helped me find a renewed core after losing myself to the myth of the perfect wife and mother.

Thank you to Michele, my surrogate sister, who lovingly

takes care of my family and me. And to Kelsey who kept me one-step ahead of office insanity.

Thank you to Eren who has been the wind beneath my wings, teaching me how to handle motherhood with grace.

And to my Laguna mom friends who feed me wine and chocolate when I need it most.

Thank you to Jan, my illustrator and friend. You have been a patient collaborator.

Thank you to my mother, who is my biggest cheerleader, and my dad, who taught me that there are no limits to what a woman can do.

Thank you to Mary Ann, my loving baby sister. She has been a faithful copy editor and a caring friend.

Most of all, thanks to my husband who has always been supportive of my creative endeavors and my beautiful daughters who remind me on a daily basis that the most important thing in life is a warm hug and a chocolate kiss.

Christine Fugate

Copyright Notices

Count Kisses, Not Calories

Visit *MotheringHeights.net*
for more essays on motherhood

Printed in the United States
111263LV00002B/223-282/P